GIVE ME THAT JOY

GIVE ME THAT JOY

A Simple Devotional Commentary
on Acts 1:1-9:31

JOHN TALLACH

Christian Focus Publications

ISBN 1 85792 263 8
© John Tallach
Cover Design by Tom Windsor
Published in
1996
by Christian Focus Publications,
Geanies House, Fearn, Ross-shire, IV20 1TW.

Contents

Copenhagen, 1838, May 19, half past ten in the morning: There is an indescribable joy which glows through us as unaccountably as the Apostle's outburst is unexpected: 'Rejoice, and again I say, Rejoice.' Not a joy over this or that, but full jubilation 'with hearts and souls and voices' ... a heavenly refrain which suddenly breaks in upon our ordinary song, a joy which cools and refreshes like a breeze, a breath of air from the trade wind which blows from the plains of Mamre to the everlasting habitations.[1]

Soren Kierkegaard

'John, Dad has been very ill during the night. He wants to speak to each of us. I think he wants to say goodbye.' So my oldest brother, Andrew, wakened me to face a dark December morning in Stornoway in 1959.

My father's face was white and his hands cold and clammy, but he had a peace about him that you could almost reach out and touch. He took my hand in his and asked: 'What would you wish to have, more than anything else in the world?'

I said nothing.

He asked again, 'Do you want to have Christ as your Saviour?'

I think I was able to make some positive response. If having Christ as my Saviour meant dying in the peace which my father was enjoying at that moment, it looked like something I could not afford to be without.

In 1960 my family moved to Dingwall, where we came under the ministry of the Rev D.A. Macfarlane. I often think with love and gratitude of the depth of the teaching he gave us, as well as the exemplary child-like grace which he exuded.

In 1979 I left the country village where I was minister to become pastor of a congregation here in Aberdeen. Someone who was a pastor in the city long before me – in fact, since 1945, the year when I was born – is the Rev William Still. He lives just two streets away. I do not go often to his door, but during a time of particular trial earlier in this year

I went to see him. There was a deep well of sympathy and understanding there, and yet a realism born of experience. There was also a deep unity which had a healing power. As I left he said with feeling, 'Well, John, why did the Lord bring us together? There must have been some purpose.' As I turned towards him the words came to me, 'Who you are is part of who I am.'

At the beginning of this book I wish to thank you,   Father of compassion and God of all comfort, for these fathers in Christ – different, yet all three so precious to me.

John Tallach,
Aberdeen
November 1996

INTRODUCTION

Will you not revive us again,
that your people may rejoice in you? (Psalm 85:6)

As George Carey, Archbishop of Canterbury, said, 'There is no escaping the note of joy in the New Testament .... Read Acts and you will see it appearing again and again. It wasn't emotionalism; it was the joy of knowing that they were forgiven people, made new through the gift of salvation and the gift of the Spirit.'[2] Or as James Denney pointed out: while some say that assurance of faith is presumption, and others say that it is a duty, in the church of the Acts 'it is simply a fact. This explains the joy which, side by side with the sense of infinite obligation, is the characteristic note of apostolic Christianity.'[3]

This joy was infectious. When the gospel moved north from Jerusalem to a city in Samaria, 'there was great joy in that city' (Acts 8:8). When the gospel moved south and an Ethiopian was converted, it was a man filled with joy who made his way back to his native country (Acts 8:39).

This joy was deep. These people were not *pretending* to be happy, while in reality they were still at war with themselves. They were not perfect, but they had learned to accept themselves through faith in Christ. They knew the seriousness of their sin; but they also knew that, in the gospel, they were called to let God's grace have the last word in their thinking, feeling and living.

In the Epistle to the Romans, Paul explains the theology
behind this joy. He says that we are justified before God, not
through who we are nor what we have done, but because of
who Christ is and through what he has done. 'Therefore,
since we have been justified through faith, we have peace
with God through our Lord Jesus Christ' (Romans 5:1). But,
in these words, Paul is not simply making a theological
statement. He is also testifying to personal experience.
Three times in the following verses he goes on to say, *we
rejoice*.

Is this part of the difference between the early church and
the church today? We know the doctrine of justification by
faith in our minds, but we do not feel the force of it in our
hearts. George Carey certainly believes that this is part of
our problem. 'In my pastoral ministry I have met so many
people, some of them convinced Evangelicals, who believe
in justification by faith with their heads, yet are condemned
by their hearts ... who have never allowed justification by
faith to be an experimental reality in their life.'[3] But if we
today can learn again the art of routing our relationship to
ourselves through Jesus Christ, will we not rediscover the
joy of the early church?

This joy was from the Holy Spirit. 'The disciples were
filled with joy *and with the Holy Spirit*' (Acts 13:52). It was
a joy 'given by the Holy Spirit' (1 Thessalonians 1:6). It was
a joy experienced 'in the Holy Spirit' (Romans 14:17).

When God revives his church, he gives this joy in a fresh
way. After the Jews returned from exile in Babylon, 'for
seven days they celebrated with joy the Feast of Unleavened
Bread, *because the Lord had filled them with joy* ....' (Ezra
6:22). The period around Pentecost was surely the most

remarkable time of revival which the church has ever experienced. No wonder that it was also a time of joy.

R. M. McCheyne, who lived in the power of the gospel himself and who personally saw revival come to congregations in Dundee and elsewhere in Scotland, said, 'Some people are afraid of anything like joy in religion. They have none themselves, and they do not love to see it in others. Their religion is something like the stars, very high, and very clear, but very cold .... May the God of hope fill you with all joy and peace in believing! If it be really in sitting under the shadow of Christ, let there be no bounds to your joy .... Rejoice in the Lord always, and again I say, Rejoice!'[4]

As we re-read the book of Acts, let us pray together: *Will you not revive us again, that your people may rejoice in you?*

1. From Luke to Acts

When he had led them out to the vicinity of Bethany, he lifted up his hands and blessed them. While he was blessing them, he left them and was taken up into heaven. Then they worshipped him and returned to Jerusalem with great joy. And they stayed continually at the temple, praising God (Luke 24:50-53).

In my former book, Theophilus, I wrote about all that Jesus began to do and to teach until the day he was taken up to heaven, after giving instructions through the Holy Spirit to the apostles he had chosen. After his suffering, he showed himself to these men and gave many convincing proofs that he was alive. He appeared to them over a period of forty days and spoke about the kingdom of God. On one occasion, while he was eating with them, he gave them this command: 'Do not leave Jerusalem, but wait for the gift my Father promised, which you have heard me speak about. For John baptised with water, but in a few days you will be baptised with the Holy Spirit.' So when they met together, they asked him, 'Lord, are you at this time going to restore the kingdom to Israel?' He said to them: 'It is not for you to know the times or dates the Father has set by his own authority. But you will receive power when the Holy Spirit comes on you; and you will be my witnesses in Jerusalem, and in all Judea and Samaria, and to the ends of the earth.' After he said this, he was taken up before their very eyes, and a cloud hid him from their sight. They were looking intently up into the sky as he was going, when suddenly two men dressed in white stood beside them. 'Men of Galilee,' they said, 'why do you stand here looking into the sky? This same Jesus, who has been taken from you into heaven, will come back in the same way you have seen him go into heaven' (Acts 1:1-11).

In Luke 1:3, the author says that his Gospel is written for Theophilus (*dear to God*).From the first verse of Acts we learn that this book, too, is written for Theophilus, and that it is the continuation of a previous volume. For these reasons, among others, Acts is taken to be written by Luke.

The Gospel began with God coming down to man in the incarnation. It ended with man, represented by Jesus, ascending up to God. At the beginning of Acts, Luke again describes Jesus' ascension into heaven. He then goes on to outline the impact which that glorious climax to our salvation had on the church and on the world.

The Blessing

The scene of Jesus' parting from his disciples lay about a mile and a half to the east of Jerusalem, at Bethany.

Jesus led the disciples out of Jerusalem, across the Kidron valley, up the slope of the Mount of Olives and a little past the shoulder of the hill.

When they had reached Bethany, Jesus turned and lifted his hands above his disciples. The priests used to do this in Old Testament times. The terms in which the blessing was given are spelt out in Numbers 6: 24-26. Now the blessing was given, not by an ordinary priest of the tribe of Levi, but by the Son of God and Saviour of sinners, who had by himself obtained eternal redemption for them. The hands that had broken the bread when the loaves were multiplied, the hands which he had placed in blessing on the little children, the hands which had been nailed to the cross, were lifted up. It was a sign that the blessing would come down. It would come down for certain because he had the right to command it.

The Parting

As he blessed them, he was parted from them. He rose from among them, and a cloud covered him from the sight of the watching disciples. It would hardly have been an ordinary cloud. There was a cloud, as a symbol of God's glory, on Mount Sinai when the Law of God was given. There was a cloud at the Transfiguration, and out of that cloud the disciples heard the voice of God. There will be clouds of glory accompanying Jesus when he will come again.

As he disappeared from view, the disciples paused to worship him. He had come as their Saviour, and in the course of working out their salvation he had suffered humiliation. Now he had shaken off all that. He had gone to his reward at God's right hand. The angels who had worshipped him at his birth would be singing his praises now, and why should the disciples not join in? He was their Saviour, he was their Lord, he was the foundation on which their whole future would be built, and they would worship him!

Think about it:

After this parting, the disciples returned to Jerusalem with great joy. How could such a painful parting end in such a positive way?

(i) Jesus had relieved their minds of a distracting question. They had been in danger of drifting off into questions of prophecy, and even of politics. But he had said to them firmly, 'That is not for you.' If we burden our minds with complicated calculations about the precise hour of our Lord's return, we are trying to carry a burden which God has not called us to bear.

(ii) He had assured them that they would meet again.

(iii) In the meantime, he had guaranteed to them his continued presence and his power. The power would come, in fulfilment of his promise, with the descent of the Holy Spirit. That power would enable them to serve their Master until his return.

Pray about it:

1. The disciples followed Jesus to Bethany. But their following of him was also at a deeper level. They followed his example and his teaching. Are we following Jesus in this way? If we follow him, we will in the end be with him where he now is.

2. What Luke described in his Gospel was only what Jesus *began* to do. The book of Acts tells the story of what Jesus went on to do, particularly in the lives of the apostles. Pray that, as you follow Jesus, his purpose will continue to be worked out in your life too.

2. What is the Secret?

Then they returned to Jerusalem from the hill called the Mount of Olives, a Sabbath day's walk from the city. When they arrived, they went upstairs to the room where they were staying. Those present were Peter, John, James and Andrew; Philip and Thomas, Bartholomew and Matthew; James son of Alphaeus and Simon the Zealot, and Judas son of James. They all joined together constantly in prayer, along with the women and Mary the mother of Jesus, and with his brothers (Acts 1:12-14).

The Book of Acts begins with a small group of people in an obscure little country in a remote corner of the Roman Empire. It ends in Rome itself, the nerve centre of the Empire where, Luke says, Paul boldly 'preached the kingdom of God and taught about the Lord Jesus Christ' (Acts 28:31). Luke does not spell out the question, but he obviously meant us to ask, 'What is the secret behind this extraordinary development – what is the explanation for this remarkable success?'

One of the answers to this question is provided in verse 14. The 'secret' is not really a secret at all. The answer is prayer, in which the affairs of the church are continually committed into the hands of the one who is able and willing to make his kingdom a reality in the world.

They were different

In his Gospel Luke tells us that, after the Ascension, the disciples were 'continually at the temple, praising God'. In Acts, he highlights their commitment to prayer of a semi-private kind. They seem to have used an upstairs room in

Jerusalem as their base. (Was it the upper room in the home of Mary, mother of John Mark, mentioned in Acts 12:12?) Whoever it belonged to, an upper room was only accessible from outside. It was a suitable venue for a group which wanted to be left in peace, undisturbed by the normal comings and goings of the household.

The disciples formed the first section in this group.

The second section was made up of women. Luke had already given a prominent place to these women in his Gospel. They had used their material resources to support Jesus' ministry (Luke 8:3); they had been present throughout his sufferings on the cross, when the disciples had been conspicuous by their absence (Luke 23:49); they were present at Jesus' burial, and prepared spices to anoint his body (Luke 23:55-56); they were first to go to the tomb on the day when he rose again, and they were the first to bear the news of his resurrection (Luke 24:1-11).

Among the women who joined these frequent prayer meetings in the upper room Luke makes particular mention of Mary, the mother of Jesus. In his Gospel, he had already dwelt on her unique importance when telling the story of Jesus' birth.

Luke's consistent emphasis on the importance of women, at a time when they were generally despised, was a contribution towards restoring to them that dignity which he knew they deserved.

The third section in the group consisted of Jesus' brothers. Some interpret this term loosely, in reference to members of his wider family rather than to children of Mary and Joseph. But there seems to be no good reason for doubting that the reference is to Jesus' brothers in the strict sense.[5] During his ministry, these brothers had not believed in him

as the promised Saviour (John 7:5). They had denounced
him as out of his mind (Mark 3:21). Now they were among
those who gathered in his name to pray for the fulfilment of
his promise. If ever there was an encouragement to perse-
vere in prayer for the conversion of those who seem hardened to the gospel, this is it.

They were united
The disciples, the women, the brothers of Jesus. They were
different, but they were united. Their hearts were fused
together as they prayed to their one Lord. What would have
helped to join them to one another?

They were united in following the pattern of Jesus'
example. In his Gospel, Luke places particular emphasis on
the importance of prayer in the life of Jesus. It is Luke who
tells us that it was as Jesus prayed that the heavens opened
and the Spirit descended on him at his baptism (Luke 3:21).
He tells us that it was as Jesus prayed that he was transfig-
ured and was covered in a heavenly glory (Luke 9:29).
Matthew and Mark tell us about Jesus' struggle in the
Garden of Gethsemane, but Luke gives us an unforgettable
picture: 'And being in anguish, he prayed more earnestly,
and his sweat was like drops of blood falling to the ground'
(Luke 22:44). It is Luke who records the fact that Jesus'
example drove the disciples to ask, 'Lord, teach us to pray'
(Luke 11:1).

They were united in rejoicing in the promise of Jesus'
presence. He had promised to be present wherever two or
three met together in his name (Matthew 18:20); he had
promised to be with his disciples to the end of the age
(Matthew 28:20).

They were united in looking forward to receiving his

power. He had promised them power (Luke 24:49, Acts
1:8). Each of those sections which made up the group in the
upper room had particular reasons for fearing that they
would lack power to be effective in the service of Christ. The
women, traditionally, had no decisive role to play. The
disciples had displayed their weakness by forsaking him at
his arrest. His brothers might have felt that, having personally refused to believe in Jesus while he was with them, they
could hardly call on others to believe in him now. Each
section of the church knew its own need, felt its own
weakness. But each section was also united to the others in
the glorious prospect of sharing an experience of God's
power.

Pray about it:
In 1967, Evelyn Christenson, the wife of a pastor in North
America, began a ministry in which she encouraged women
to pray in groups. Here are some of the lessons which she,
and the others who joined with her, learned from their
experiences.

1. If we are to meet together for effective prayer, we must
ourselves be right with God. We must be free, for example,
from pretence, from pride, and from divided motives.[6]

2. If we are to meet together for effective prayer, we must
have all spiritual barriers between one another removed.
Evelyn was deeply experienced in her ministry of encouraging other women to form prayer groups when she found that
she herself had to learn this lesson in a fresh way. She tells
how she joined a group of women to pray about a financial
crisis, and expresses frankly her thoughts on meeting one
member of that group. Evelyn thought, looking at her
clothes and listening to her talk, 'She's the squarest woman

I've ever seen in my life.' But then, 'I suddenly realised that
I was about to spend my morning in prayer for these
financial needs with sin in my heart.' When this stranger
prayed, Evelyn says, 'I realised that this woman had a
dimension to her prayer life that I knew nothing about ... I
felt two inches high.'[7]

3. If we are to meet together for effective prayer, we must
learn to present *requests*, not answers. This means that we
are genuinely open to God's will for us. Far from approaching him with solutions to which we cling through thick and
thin, our perception of his will for us may change dramatically as we wait on him. We may come at first with an
external problem, thinking that what is needed is for God to
effect some change in that situation. We may well find,
however, that the purpose of the external problem is to
highlight another problem within ourselves. We then move
on to realise that it is us who need to be changed, and this
becomes the focus of our prayers.

3. Three Personalities

In those days Peter stood up among the believers (a group numbering about a hundred and twenty) and said, 'Brothers, the Scripture had to be fulfilled which the Holy Spirit spoke long ago through the mouth of David concerning Judas, who served as guide for those who arrested Jesus – he was one of our number and shared in this ministry.' (With the reward he got for his wickedness, Judas bought a field; there he fell headlong, his body burst open and all his intestines spilled out. Everyone in Jerusalem heard about this, so they called that field in their language Akeldama, that is, Field of Blood.) 'For,' said Peter, 'it is written in the book of Psalms, "May his place be deserted; let there be no one to dwell in it," and "May another take his place of leadership." Therefore it is necessary to choose one of the men who have been with us the whole time the Lord Jesus went in and out among us, beginning from John's baptism to the time when Jesus was taken up from us. For one of these must become a witness with us of his resurrection.' So they proposed two men: Joseph called Barsabbas (also known as Justus) and Matthias. Then they prayed, 'Lord, you know everyone's heart. Show us which of these two you have chosen to take over this apostolic ministry, which Judas left to go where he belongs.' Then they cast lots, and the lot fell to Matthias; so he was added to the eleven apostles (Acts 1:15-26; cf. Matthew 27:3-10).

There are three personalities in this closing section of the first chapter of Acts – Peter, Judas, and Matthias.

Peter
Luke has told us about Peter's flagrant denial of his Lord. He has also told us about Jesus' prior commitment to pray for

Peter's restoration (Luke 22:31-32). This restoration, when it came, had a private and a public aspect.

The private meeting is mentioned in Luke 24:34 and in 1 Corinthians 15:5.

The story of Peter's public restoration to office is given in John 21:15-17. Three times Peter had denied Jesus. Three times Jesus asked Peter if he loved him, and three times confirmed his appointment as a shepherd over the church: 'Feed my sheep.'

So Peter's calling was not ruined for ever by his fall. By God's miraculous grace, he was still able to take responsibility for the affairs of the church. If we have fallen, we may be tempted to believe that we have no future in the service of Christ. But we have to leave that to him. In fact a painful experience of our own weakness (when this is followed by repentance) can make us more rather than less useful in the church.

Judas

As Peter said (verse 17), Judas was given the privilege of having the same office as the other eleven disciples. He preached the gospel. We must also assume that God worked with healing power through Judas, as he worked through the eleven, otherwise the others would have had reason to suspect him. As it was, instead of suspecting him they placed unusual trust in him by allowing him to administer their financial affairs.

But Judas betrayed the trust which was placed in him. Peter did not dwell on this. His language was restrained. Judas, Peter said, was 'guide for those who arrested Jesus'. Perhaps the painful awareness of his own fall kept Peter back from dwelling on Judas' treachery.

What Peter did emphasise was that, even in relation to this tragedy, the 'Scripture had to be fulfilled which the Holy Spirit spoke'. He then went on to use the Old Testament to make two points. The first point was that Judas had to fall from his office because the Scripture had foretold this (Psalm 69:25). The second point, again because this was indicated in Scripture (Psalm 109:8), was that someone had to take the place left vacant by the traitor.

At this juncture Luke inserts into his narrative some details regarding the death of Judas. On the surface, these details seem to be out of harmony with some elements in the account given by Matthew. It is, however, possible to harmonise the two versions of Judas' end.

First of all, the fact that Judas hanged himself (as Matthew tells us) is not in conflict with the details which Luke supplies here about Judas' body falling to the ground and rupturing. Again, Luke represents Peter as saying that Judas himself bought a field with the money he received for betraying Jesus; whereas Matthew says that it was the priests who bought a field with this money after Judas, filled with remorse, had returned the thirty pieces of silver to them. But surely Peter could feel free to give his account in a way which made a particular point (rather than simply going over facts with which his audience were already familiar). His point was that Judas derived no benefit from this payment which had meant so much to him. All Judas got from it was a field which became a burying place for strangers. This lonely cemetery became a powerful picture of how unprofitable it is for any of us to sin against God.

As to how that field came to be named – there seems no reason why two factors could not have combined to fix on that place the name 'The field of blood'. It was blood money which purchased the field; and in that field the blood of the betrayer himself was spilt.

Matthias

Matthias was one of the two present in the company of 120 who were nominated for taking Judas' place. The qualification mentioned was that he could personally testify to the facts of Jesus' ministry, from the time when John the Baptist introduced Jesus to the world to the time when Jesus ascended to heaven.

That was an outward qualification. His inward qualification – the state of his heart – was a matter which God alone could judge.

So, committing this important transaction into the hands of God, that group of believers used an Old Testament method for discerning God's will. It seems likely that this involved marking two stones, one for Matthias and another for Barsabas, placing these stones in a vessel and shaking the vessel till one of the stones flew out. After the Spirit descended, this method of seeking guidance would not be mentioned again in the New Testament.

Think about it:
Judas got thirty pieces of silver for betraying Jesus. But his loss was greater, and more lasting, than his gain.

In 1994, a thief stole six dollars from a restaurant in Rio De Janeiro. However, in his hurry to get away, he left his jacket behind. The wallet in his jacket contained eighty dollars!

Whenever we sin, our loss is greater than our gain.

Pray about it:

1. We may be concerned that we will deny Jesus, as Peter did, or even betray him as Judas did. But the important question is, What is our heart relationship to Jesus? Do we look for the mercy of God to shine on us through him? Do we follow him, in obedience to his commandments? If so, we can be assured that we will 'through faith' be 'shielded by God's power' (1 Peter 1:5).

2. There may have been others qualified to take Judas' place, who were not present when the early church felt led to appoint Judas' successor. Do we sometimes miss out on God's calling because we are not as involved in the affairs of his church as we should be?

4. The Descent of the Spirit

When the day of Pentecost came, they were all together in one place. Suddenly a sound like the blowing of a violent wind came from heaven and filled the whole house where they were sitting. They saw what seemed to be tongues of fire that separated and came to rest on each of them. All of them were filled with the Holy Spirit and began to speak in other tongues as the Spirit enabled them (Acts 2:1-4).

Passover and Pentecost

Before his ascension, Jesus had assured his disciples that they would be baptised with the Spirit 'in a few days'. Ten days later, on the Day of Pentecost, that promise was fulfilled.

'Pentecost' is from the Greek word for fiftieth. The Jews counted fifty days from the day after the Sabbath after the Passover. That is how, following Leviticus 23, they calculated when the Day of Pentecost fell.

The Passover was celebrated on the fourteenth day of April. The day after the Sabbath following the Passover was counted as the first day of the barley harvest. To mark that day, a sheaf from the first barley to be harvested was presented as an offering before God.

Pentecost, fifty days after that first day of harvest, was marked by the presentation before God of two barley loaves (Leviticus 23:17).

The fact that the Passover (when Jesus died) and Pentecost (when the Spirit came) were linked is an illustration for us of how the work of Jesus and the work of the Spirit are bound up together. In fact it shows us (without wishing to push the parallel too far) that although the raw materials of our salvation were all in place by the time Jesus had finished his work, we need the Spirit to come before we can benefit from that work. The gospel alone is like a sheaf of grain, which has the potential to feed us. The gospel in the hands of the Spirit is like a loaf of bread, in which the saving work of Christ comes to us in a way which we can absorb, in a form which can satisfy our hunger.

The signs of the Spirit

The first sign of the Spirit's coming was a sound like the noise of a roaring wind. Ezekiel had used the wind as a symbol of the Spirit in chapter 37 of his prophecy. Jesus did the same in his conversation with Nicodemus in John chapter 3.

A fortnight before the time of writing, the power of the wind was felt all over Britain. One friend in a village in north west Scotland told me what things were like on a particular day. The first thing she noticed after wakening that morning was, the noise of the wind roaring round the house. Two caravans parked beside her neighbour's house had been smashed up. A brick had come crashing through the window of his house. Outside his house, lying here and there on the hillside, were pieces of the roof from the fish market down at the pier, quarter of a mile away. The wind had wrenched off these sections of the roof and had carried them clear across the harbour!

Nearer home here in Aberdeen, a man in Gardenstown had his car blown over a wall and thrown down a cliff into the sea. One night he parked his yellow Mini safely outside his house. The next morning he found it sitting in the sea, with the waves up to the windows. Only the wind had done it.

When the Spirit comes, he can change things dramatically. He can smash up churches. He can put a brick through the window of a church, and introduce a sudden rush of fresh air. He can tear the roofs off churches, or blow down their walls. He can suddenly redesign them in a radical and irreversible way.

Then there appeared tongues of fire. Fire had been a symbol of God's presence in the burning bush, and on Mount Sinai. John the Baptist had promised of Jesus, 'He will baptise you with the Holy Spirit and with fire' (Luke 3:16).

Parallels
There are parallels between Luke's account of the baptism of Jesus in his Gospel, and his account in Acts of the baptism of the New Testament church on the day of Pentecost. Both events were preceded by prayer (Luke 3:21, Acts 1:14). There were two signs of God's presence at Jesus' baptism – the voice from heaven a witness to men's ears, and the dove a witness to their eyes. So, at the baptism of the early church in Acts 2, the presence of the Spirit was attested by the sound of the wind and by the sight of the fire.

Also, at his baptism, Jesus was filled with the Holy Spirit (Luke 4:1). Similarly, the believers who gathered together on the Day of Pentecost were filled with the Holy Spirit.

Sweet wine
Later on (verse 13), Luke tells us that the early church was charged with drunkenness. Drunkenness induces a kind of merriment, a closeness between drinkers, a courage to tackle impossible tasks. From the charge of drunkenness we may deduce that the early church displayed some of these

characteristics. There was a joy, there was a sense of belonging to one another, there was an optimism about fulfilling their calling to witness to their Lord.

But the cause of this condition was not alcohol, but the Holy Spirit. They had drunk deeply of him. They were filled with the Spirit. This was the source of the infectious, world-conquering joy of the early church.

Think about it:

Jesus rose from the dead on the day after the Sabbath following the Passover. The fact that he rose on that day – when the first ripe sheaf of the barley harvest was presented before God – lies behind Paul's statement in 1 Corinthians 15:20: 'Christ has indeed been raised from the dead, the first fruits of those who have fallen asleep.' The presentation of the first ripe sheaf was a promise of the full harvest yet to come. So the resurrection of Christ is a guarantee that all who believe in him will also rise from the dead, as he did.

Pray about it:

1. Thinking of the link between Passover and Pentecost, and the link between the work of Christ and of the Spirit, how much do we ask the Spirit to help us really benefit from the work of Christ?

2. Fire is a symbol of the Spirit's purity. How willing are we to endure the pain which the Spirit's purifying fire can bring?

3. Wind is a symbol of the Spirit's power. Even an insignificant implement can become very effective, when lifted up by the power of the wind. How much do we pray that our service, which in itself is weak, will become effective as it is taken up in the power of the Spirit?

4. In Ephesians 5:18 we are told not to be drunk with wine, but to be filled with the Spirit. The early church was filled with the Spirit. Believers yielded themselves up to his control, giving rise to the charge that they were under the influence of alcohol. When were we last so filled with the Spirit that we would give the least grounds for such a charge?

5. The Church Moves Out

Now there were staying in Jerusalem God-fearing Jews from every nation under heaven. When they heard this sound, a crowd came together in bewilderment, because each one heard them speaking in his own language. Utterly amazed, they asked: 'Are not all these men who are speaking Galileans? Then how is it that each of us hears them in his own native language? Parthians, Medes and Elamites; residents of Mesopotamia, Judea and Cappadocia, Pontus and Asia, Phrygia and Pamphylia, Egypt and the parts of Libya near Cyrene; visitors from Rome (both Jews and converts to Judaism); Cretans and Arabs – we hear them declaring the wonders of God in our own tongues!' Amazed and perplexed, they asked one another, 'What does this mean?' Some, however, made fun of them and said, 'They have had too much wine' (Acts 2:5-13).

The focus of attention now shifts from the Spirit-filled church to those outside.

From the farthest corners

At the Feast of Pentecost, thousands of Jews from around the world made a pilgrimage to Jerusalem. Luke gives us a list of countries from which they had come on this occasion. They had come from the area of modern Iraq and Iran. They had come from various Roman provinces in modern Turkey. Some had come from Egypt, Libya and Cyrene in North Africa, and there were visitors from Rome. Lastly Luke mentions visitors from the island of Crete as well as from Arabia to the east of Judea. There does not seem to be much order to his list – as if he was so excited at the presence of these visitors that he could not list them in an orderly way! It was exciting, because all these visitors to the capital of the Jewish world had the potential to bring the gospel of Christ back to the farthest corners from which they had come.

What was it that stirred up their interest? The believers, full of the Spirit, were testifying to 'the wonders of God' (verse 11). But what particularly arrested the attention of these pilgrims was the fact that, although the believers in Jerusalem were presumably speaking Aramaic, the members of the crowd heard what was being said in their own language. We don't know exactly how this happened. Perhaps one believer was being heard in the language of Libya, and those who spoke that language congregated around him. Then, when another believer was being heard in the language of Elam, those from that country gathered around him.

Unity in diversity
It was a miracle of unity in diversity. The church was speaking of the central facts of God's salvation, but this testimony was being heard in many languages. It was, in a sense, a reversal of Babel (Genesis 11:1-9). Then, because of man's sin, society was divided and communication barriers went up. Now, because of God's grace, these divisions were healed and the barriers of communication came down.

Yet the validity and value of each culture was upheld. These people did not have to discard their own culture and the language in which that culture was expressed in order to hear the gospel, or to become Christians. The Holy Spirit brought the gospel to them, wrapped up in their own native speech. In this, as in other respects, Christianity stands apart from Islam. To those born outside of Islam, if they wish to become Muslims they must accept that their native language and culture are inferior to the Arabic culture and language in which Islam was born. But on the day of Pentecost, it was the Spirit of God who overcame the barriers of culture and language in his eagerness to get across the gospel of Christ.

Luke does not explain how the believers moved out of where they were and joined the crowd outside. All we know is that, at some stage, the church moved out. One hundred and twenty believers, filled with the Spirit but only making God's praises bounce off the walls of a private room, would not have accomplished much. The same number, drawn out into the open so as to interact with that mixed crowd of needy people meant that the scene was set for turning the world upside down.

Think about it:
The gift of tongues, which the Spirit gave to the church on the day of Pentecost, was a clear indication that the Spirit had come on believers to enable them to evangelise the world. The tongues spoken were the languages of real people. (Mere incoherent speech would have supported the charge of drunkenness – a charge which Peter was anxious to repudiate.)

The Spirit's message through the gift of tongues was – *I will give you the power to take the good news about Jesus to all the other language groups in the world. In fact some of them are in Jerusalem at this moment. You can begin your worldwide mission by bringing the gospel to them here and now.*

Pray about it:

1. Jesus told his disciples that, when the Spirit would come, he would convict the world (John 16:8). How much do we consciously look to the Spirit to do, though perhaps through us, what we can never accomplish by ourselves?

2. It was because the church was filled with the Spirit that they were able to move out into the stream of life in Jerusalem at this busy time of the Feast and witness effectively to 'the wonders of God'. Pray that the church would again be filled, and go on being filled with the Spirit, so that we would be eased out of our backwaters. Mixing effectively with those outside we would give them the opportunity to receive, through us, what they so desperately need.

6. Preaching at Pentecost

The preacher

> Then Peter stood up with the Eleven, raised his voice and addressed the crowd: 'Fellow Jews and all of you who are in Jerusalem, let me explain this to you; listen carefully to what I say' (Acts 2:14).

If any special proof were needed that the Spirit had descended on the church, Peter himself was that proof. All the disciples had denied their Lord, but Peter had fallen more dramatically than the others. Now he was standing up, at this crucial point in the development of the early church, and speaking with grace, with authority and with great skill.

The introduction

> 'These men are not drunk, as you suppose. It's only nine in the morning! No, this is what was spoken by the prophet Joel: "In the last days, God says, I will pour out my Spirit on all people. Your sons and daughters will prophesy, your young men will see visions, your old men will dream dreams. Even on my servants, both men and women, I will pour out my Spirit in those days, and they will prophesy. I will show wonders in the heaven above and signs on the earth below, blood and fire and billows of smoke. The sun will be turned to darkness and the moon to blood before the coming of the great and glorious day of the Lord. And everyone who calls on the name of the Lord will be saved"' (Acts 2:15-21).

Peter dealt first with the idea that the believers were under
the influence of alcohol. He disposed of this suggestion like
a seasoned politician. He did not get bogged down, defending the church in a laborious way. The allegation got the
brisk, perhaps even humorous, dismissal that it needed.

Then Peter invited his audience to take another view
altogether of what was happening. He told them that,
hundreds of years before, God had foretold these developments through his prophet Joel. In quoting Joel 2:28-32,
Peter communicated the fact that his message was rooted in
God's Word. Given that his audience was made up of devout
Jews, he was also introducing his subject in a framework
with which his hearers were familiar and for which they had
the highest respect.

The passage from Joel held out the prospect of an
abundant outpouring of God's Spirit. This was a precious oil
which, in Old Testament times, was measured out in drops
to a few. But now, in these 'last days', God was to give out
his Spirit with generosity. He was not to limit this gift to an
elite band of prophets, but was to pour him out on 'all
people'.

The old were to receive him, but also the young. Men
were to receive him, but also women. The rich were to
receive him, but also the poor. Distinctions of age, sex and
social or economic advantage were to be disregarded. In
fact, the outpouring of the Spirit would to some extent
sweep these distinctions away.

The reference to portents and signs towards the end of the
passage from Joel gives more than a flavour of God's
coming judgment. (Old Testament prophecy tended not to
distinguish between the first coming of Christ to save and
his second coming to judge. Perhaps this helps us to under-

stand why John the Baptist stumbled at one stage over accepting Jesus as the Messiah. John saw Jesus' ministry to be replete with works of grace, but where was the note of judgment which he had learned to expect? At that stage John did not realise that the Old Testament prophecies of judgment would be fulfilled when Jesus would come again.)

Against this background of judgement in Joel's prophecy, there was a clear presentation of God's grace: 'everyone who calls on the name of the Lord will be saved'. By the 'Lord' of Joel's prophecy the Jews would understand 'Yahweh' – the name by which God had revealed himself to the Jews in the Old Testament. That same 'Lord' had come near again in the person and work of Jesus. In fact the 'Lord' and 'Jesus' were one. Anyone therefore who made application to Jesus, acknowledging him as Lord, would receive salvation directly and personally from him. Salvation from judgement, salvation to eternal life, for anyone who cast himself on the mercy of God in Jesus Christ! The promise which God had given in Joel 2:32 was like a book of cheques which he had signed. Anyone who, believing in Jesus as the Saviour whom God had promised, signed his name where God had left the word 'everyone' would immediately possess the riches of his grace.

Pray about it:
1. In the passage which Peter quoted from Joel there is a call to repentance – a call to church leaders to weep, a call to the people to rend their hearts (Joel 2:12 f.). Is there any sin in our hearts or lives which may be acting as a restraint on the outpouring of the Spirit today?

2. The portents in that passage which give more than a hint of judgement also proclaim the fact that the day of

God's coming will be a day of radical and irreversible change. (Although Peter did to some extent understand this, time would tell that he was in fact reluctant to face the depth and breadth of the changes which Pentecost had brought.) Are we prepared for the fact that, when the Spirit comes, he may call us to face changes with which we may find it difficult to cope?

7. The Main Message

'Men of Israel, listen to this: Jesus of Nazareth was a man accredited by God to you by miracles, wonders and signs, which God did among you through him, as you yourselves know. This man was handed over to you by God's set purpose and foreknowledge; and you, with the help of wicked men, put him to death by nailing him to the cross. But God raised him from the dead, freeing him from the agony of death, because it was impossible for death to keep its hold on him. David said about him: "I saw the Lord always before me. Because he is at my right hand, I will not be shaken. Therefore my heart is glad and my tongue rejoices; my body also will live in hope, because you will not abandon me to the grave, nor will you let your Holy One see decay. You have made known to me the paths of life; you will fill me with joy in your presence." Brothers, I can tell you confidently that the patriarch David died and was buried, and his tomb is here to this day. But he was a prophet and knew that God had promised him on oath that he would place one of his descendants on his throne. Seeing what was ahead, he spoke of the resurrection of the Christ, that he was not abandoned to the grave, nor did his body see decay. God has raised this Jesus to life, and we are all witnesses of the fact. Exalted to the right hand of God, he has received from the Father the promised Holy Spirit and has poured out what you now see and hear. For David did not ascend to heaven, and yet he said, "The Lord said to my Lord: Sit at my right hand until I make your enemies a footstool for your feet." Therefore let all Israel be assured of this: God has made this Jesus, whom you crucified, both Lord and Christ' (Acts 2:22-36).

The main theme of this Pentecost sermon is Jesus. He is like the hub of a wheel, from which the spokes go out in different directions. Jesus is the centre and the strength of this sermon, without which it would fall apart. In the course of his sermon Peter moves out from and back to his central theme in three directions.

His hearers' contacts with Jesus

1. Peter's hearers knew Jesus. His ministry was not conducted in some far-away corner, but on their doorsteps. They knew about the wonderful works with which God had attested the ministry of Jesus. They had known for some time about the healings; they had heard about the raising of Lazarus from the dead at Bethany, less than two miles from Jerusalem.

2. Peter's hearers crucified Jesus. Those who prided themselves in knowing the law of God had laid hands unlawfully on the Son of God, and put him to death.

3. Peter now confronted his hearers with the evidence of Jesus' ongoing activity. What they attributed to drunkenness was actually to be attributed to the Holy Spirit whom Jesus had sent from his position of authority at God's right hand. 'He poured out what you now see and hear.' The very one whom they had killed was still around, and was still confronting them with his claims!

Jesus and Old Testament prophecy

To set the work of the Spirit in context, Peter referred his hearers to the Prophecy of Joel. To set the person and work of Jesus in context, he referred to two passages from the Book of Psalms. Presenting his message in this way, Peter honoured two important principles of preaching at the same time. He demonstrated to his hearers the fact that his message was not the product of his own brain but was derived from the word of God. Also, he presented his message in a framework with which his hearers were familiar. To a Gentile audience, these passages of Scripture would have sounded strange. But Peter's Jewish hearers were intimately acquainted with them, and accepted them as authoritative.

Peter's use of both Psalm 16 and Psalm 110 was very simple. First of all, he showed that what was said in these prophetic Psalms was not fulfilled in David himself, who wrote them. David did not tabernacle temporarily in the realm of the departed, as Psalm 16 foretold. David did not ascend up to God's right hand, as Psalm 110 prophesied. Secondly, Peter said, the prophecies which were not fulfilled in David himself were fulfilled in Jesus. Therefore, Peter concluded, Jesus is the Lord's anointed whose resurrection was foretold in Psalm 16 and whose ascension to glory was foretold in Psalm 110.

Jesus and the God of Israel

Again, Peter made three points about the relationship between Jesus and the God whom his hearers professed to follow.

Firstly, through many miracles, wonders and signs, God had proclaimed in the most powerful and public way that Jesus was his servant and his Son.

Secondly, even though in the death of Jesus there was an outbreak of lawlessness on a massive scale, God was still ruling in these events. In fact, it was God himself who had planned and appointed them.

Thirdly, God raised Jesus from the dead. Peter loved to

set these two things as close together as possible – men did
Jesus down to death, but God raised him up from the dead
(see Acts 2:23-24; 3:14-15; 4:10; 10:39-40).

Pray about it:
Peter charged his hearers with murdering the Son of God.
Yet, in the course of his sermon, he seemed to move closer
to his hearers instead of distancing himself from them. From
calling them 'men of Israel' in verse 22, he progressed to
calling them 'brothers' in verse 29.

Pray that those involved in communicating the gospel
today will be helped by the Holy Spirit, as Peter was, so that
they also will do this in a loving and effective way.

8. The Impact

Pierced to the heart

> When the people heard this, they were cut to the heart and said
> to Peter and the other apostles, 'Brothers, what shall we do?'
> (Acts 2:37).

Peter had told his hearers about the kind of Messiah God had
promised. He had shown them that Jesus was precisely that
Messiah. Then he had charged them with murdering him.

The effect of this on Peter's hearers was devastating.
They were pierced to the heart. Jesus had promised that,
when the Spirit would come, he would convict the world of
sin (John 16:8). Peter preached in the power of the Spirit on
the Day of Pentecost, and this was the result. The message
penetrated all their defences.

Such dramatic conviction of sin has occurred often,
when the Spirit has accompanied the preaching of the gospel
with particular power. David Brainerd describes in his diary
what happened when he preached the gospel to the Red
Indians at Crossweeksung in 1745. 'Some could neither go
nor stand, but lay flat on the ground, as if pierced at heart,
crying incessantly for mercy.'[8] Peter's hearers did not argue
with anything he had said. Instead, they turned to him for
help: 'What shall we do?'

Peter's response

> Peter replied, 'Repent and be baptised, every one of you, in the
> name of Jesus Christ for the forgiveness of your sins. And you
> will receive the gift of the Holy Spirit. The promise is for you

and your children and for all who are far off – for all whom the
Lord our God will call.' With many other words he warned
them; and he pleaded with them, 'Save yourselves from this
corrupt generation.' Those who accepted his message were
baptised, and about three thousand were added to their number
that day (Acts 2:38-41).

First, Peter called for a change. That is what repentance
means – a profound change in attitude and behaviour.

Next, Peter called for a commitment to Christ. In one
sense, this is a private thing. But Peter asked for this inner
commitment to be expressed publicly, through the sacrament of baptism.

Such a sacrament, like the baptism which John the
Baptist had administered, meant that the participant committed himself into the hands of God for the washing away
of his sins.

Where this was done sincerely, looking in faith to Jesus
through whom alone cleansing can come, Peter assured his
hearers of two things. Sin would be washed away. The
sinner would be released from his guilt like a person
discharged from a debt, or like a prisoner set free from his
prison. Positively, those who repented and believed would
receive the gift of the Holy Spirit.

To drive home this good news, Peter reaffirmed the
gospel promise to which the Israelites had held on throughout the Old Testament period. This promise had endured
from generation to generation. It was now extended without
limit of distance, 'to all who are far off'. Whatever stranger
was in Jerusalem that day, from the ends of the earth, he
could claim this promise for himself.

Many received his words, and many responded. Before

the sun went down beyond the Mediterranean Sea that night, three thousand souls in Jerusalem had been added to the church.

Pray about it:

1. If there is guilt on your conscience, look directly to the Saviour whom Peter presented to his hearers on the Day of Pentecost, and receive the same cleansing as they received.

2. Pray that, wherever the gospel is preached today, the Spirit will convict men of their need, and persuade them to accept forgiveness as a gift from God, as he did when Peter preached that day in Jerusalem.

9. The Church Goes on with God

They devoted themselves to the apostles' teaching and to the fellowship, to the breaking of bread and to prayer. Everyone was filled with awe, and many wonders and miraculous signs were done by the apostles. All the believers were together and had everything in common. Selling their possessions and goods, they gave to anyone as he had need. Every day they continued to meet together in the temple courts. They broke bread in their homes and ate together with glad and sincere hearts, praising God and enjoying the favour of all the people. And the Lord added to their number daily those who were being saved (Acts 2:42-47).

Here is a verbal picture of the dynamic spiritual life of the early church, as it went on with God.

What were they doing?
The blessings of Pentecost were not a flash in the pan. The church which was so blessed and so enlarged that day went on to demonstrate in different ways the reality of the blessings it had received.

They persevered. They stuck to the apostles' teaching, and they stuck to one another. They showed their adherence to one another by their continued coming together for the Lord's Supper, for prayer, and for praise. At the stated times of prayer in the temple, and at other times in their own homes, they met frequently each day.

They also demonstrated their commitment to one another in the most practical way. Many of those who had possessions sold them. This practice took hold in the early church because of the deep love and the practical concern which believers felt for one another. There were specific requirements in the Old Testament about caring for the poor. But, with the descent of the Spirit, the care of New Testament believers for one another overflowed far beyond the letter of the law.

What was God doing?
God continued to demonstrate the heavenly source of all this by wonders and signs which kindled a fear, or awe, in those outside the church. The love which was so evidently ruling the lives of believers must also have been used by God to communicate to unbelievers the reality of what was going on.

So the church just kept on growing. More and more people were brought in from outside, to experience for themselves God's saving power.

Pray about it:
1. Pray for the work of God's Spirit within the church, creating a commitment to prayer, praise, and a practical concern for one another.

2. Pray for the work of God's Spirit outwith the church, bringing home to the hearts of many the reality of what God is doing within the church, and bringing them to seek salvation for themselves.

10. The Sign

One day Peter and John were going up to the temple at the time of prayer – at three in the afternoon. Now a man crippled from birth was being carried to the temple gate called Beautiful, where he was put every day to beg from those going into the temple courts. When he saw Peter and John about to enter, he asked them for money. Peter looked straight at him, as did John. Then Peter said, 'Look at us!' So the man gave them his attention, expecting to get something from them. Then Peter said, 'Silver and gold I do not have, but what I have I give you. In the name of Jesus Christ of Nazareth, walk.' Taking him by the right hand, he helped him up, and instantly the man's feet and ankles became strong. He jumped to his feet and began to walk. Then he went with them into the temple courts, walking and jumping, and praising God. When all the people saw him walking and praising God, they recognised him as the same man who used to sit begging at the temple gate called Beautiful, and they were filled with wonder and amazement at what had happened to him (Acts 3:1-10).

This miracle of healing is given by Luke as an example of the many 'wonders and signs' (2:43) which were done at this time through the apostles. By means of these miracles God set his seal on the gospel preached by the apostles, just as he had done on the preaching of his Son.

Old friends

Luke tells us that Peter and John went up to the temple together. They had been friends for a long time. They had fished together, they had been together on the Mount of Transfiguration, they had been close to Jesus in the Garden of Gethsemane. They had gone together to the house of the High Priest the night when Peter denied Jesus, they had run together to his tomb on the morning of the third day. They had been together when Jesus, by the Sea of Galilee, gave Peter three opportunities to express his ongoing love for him.

And they were still together, going up to the temple around three in the afternoon, to be present at the time of prayer which accompanied the offering of the evening sacrifice.

More than money

The Beautiful Gate seems to have led from the Court of the Gentiles into the Court of the Women. As Peter and John climbed the stairs from the Court of the Gentiles towards the Beautiful Gate, they came across this lame man whom his friends were just depositing in front of the gate. It was a prime position for his trade. Worshippers, passing through the gate to attend prayers, would feel obliged to give him charity.

The lame man began to beg immediately, directing his efforts towards Peter and John. Peter did not excuse himself and hurry on, for fear that the time of prayer would start without him. He gave this man his full attention.

The beggar thought that he was about to receive money. Peter told him that he did not have any money to give. However, what he did have he was willing to give.

Jesus had told the disciples that, after his ascent to his Father, the church would do even greater miracles than had been accomplished during his lifetime. He gave that promise in John 14:12. In the following verse he said, 'I will do whatever you ask in my name, so that the Son may bring glory to the Father.' This suggests that these miracles would be performed in answer to the church's prayers, offered in the name of Jesus. No doubt Peter and John, standing on the steps beside the lame beggar, offered such prayer. In that atmosphere of prayer, in the strength of the Spirit, Peter said, 'Rise up and walk.' Only because he had faith in him through whom God had revealed himself did he dare to hold out this hope. And he did hold it out. Sympathising with the man, and assured that God would meet his need, he touched this beggar. In the certain expectation that God would grant immediate healing, he helped the man to his feet.

For the first time in forty years, the man stood up. He took a step forward. Then, walking was not good enough for a man who had something to celebrate. He leapt into the air. And on he went, thrilled with his new found freedom, taking a few steps, leaping, and praising the God from whom this gift had come.

Pray about it:

1. John had witnessed at close quarters how Peter had denied his Lord. He could have gossiped against his brother all over Jerusalem. Instead, he showed that love which keeps no score of wrongs. Pray that Christian leaders would forgive one another and support one another's ministries, as John did for Peter.

2. The lame beggar who asked Peter and John for charity on the steps of the temple is a picture of those outside the church who look to us for help. We are in danger of pressing on with the worship of God, while ignoring those whose pained eyes look in hope in our direction. Pray that the church today will be guided and strengthened by the Spirit to respond in the best way to the need of those outside.

11. The Sermon

The setting

> While the beggar held on to Peter and John, all the people were astonished and came running to them in the place called Solomon's Colonnade. When Peter saw this, he said to them: 'Men of Israel, why does this surprise you? Why do you stare at us as if by our own power or godliness we had made this man walk?' (Acts 3:11-12).

After evening prayers, the healed cripple could not forget the wonderful blessing he had received that day. Nor could he forget those through whom this blessing had come to him. In fact, he followed them everywhere.

This served to keep alive, and even to increase, the impact of the miracle on the crowd. As the congregation streamed out into the Court of the Women, they swung over to the left and filled up what was called Solomon's Colonnade. This was to the east side of the Court of the Women. Three rows of pillars provided a vast covered area where people could gather. Jesus himself had on occasion taught here (John 10:23).

A huge crowd was gathering, and a deep sense was filling them that something truly miraculous had just taken place. Peter perceived that God had set this scene for the preaching of the gospel, and he was not about to miss his opportunity.

The substance

> 'The God of Abraham, Isaac and Jacob, the God of our fathers, has glorified his servant Jesus. You handed him over to be killed, and you disowned him before Pilate, though he had decided to let him go. You disowned the Holy and Righteous

One and asked that a murderer be released to you. You killed the author of life, but God raised him from the dead. We are witnesses of this. By faith in the name of Jesus, this man whom you see and know was made strong. It is Jesus' name and the faith that comes through him that has given this complete healing to him, as you can all see' (Acts 3:13-16).

First he told the crowd to stop staring at himself and John. The secret of the miracle did not lie with them.

Then he pointed to God, presenting him in such a way as to maximise the common ground between himself and his hearers. It was not some strange power but the familiar 'God of our fathers' who had done this miraculous thing.

But some background was required. Behind the miracle of healing which had taken place at the Beautiful Gate that day lay the miraculous raising of Jesus from the dead. Speaking of the death of Jesus involved speaking of the sin of those who killed him, and Peter did not dodge round this point.

Jesus was the 'Servant of the Lord' whose coming had been foretold by the Old Testament prophets, like Isaiah. This Jesus Peter's hearers had dragged up before a pagan ruler. They had rejected the Lord's chosen servant, even when Pilate had wanted to let him go. Rejecting him who was righteous, they chose instead a murderer. Surely here was the ultimate spewing out of the wickedness of the human heart – they did down to death him who had been appointed by God as the source of all life.

But it was not their evil verdict which stood. God raised him from the dead.

Having supplied that essential bit of background, Peter returned to the miracle of healing. It had nothing to do with magical powers or special piety. It was through faith in

Jesus, this servant of the Lord whom God had vindicated by raising him from the dead, that the man who had been a cripple for forty years had been healed in Jerusalem that day.

The personal application

'Now, brothers, I know that you acted in ignorance, as did your leaders. But this is how God fulfilled what he had foretold through all the prophets, saying that his Christ would suffer. Repent, then, and turn to God, so that your sins may be wiped out, that times of refreshing may come from the Lord, and that he may send the Christ, who has been appointed for you – even Jesus. He must remain in heaven until the time comes for God to restore everything, as he promised long ago through his holy prophets. For Moses said, "The Lord your God will raise up for you a prophet like me from among your own people; you must listen to everything he tells you. Anyone who does not listen to him will be completely cut off from among his people." Indeed, all the prophets from Samuel on, as many as have spoken, have foretold these days. And you are heirs of the prophets and of the covenant God made with your fathers. He said to Abraham, "Through your offspring all peoples on earth will be blessed." When God raised up his servant, he sent him first to you to bless you by turning each of you from your wicked ways' (Acts 3:17-26).

President Ford was once impressed by a sermon, and afterwards spoke to the preacher. 'That was a fine sermon you preached,' he said. 'But if you worked for me I would fire you.' The preacher asked why, and the president replied, 'Because you told me, and you sold me, but you did not sign me up.' President Ford could not have made that criticism of Peter, preaching in Solomon's Colonnade.

Having charged his hearers with murdering the Lord of Life, Peter said he knew that they did it in ignorance. There was a sense in which they did know what they were doing. But Peter's aim was to hold out to them the prospect of forgiveness, and it would have been counterproductive to dwell now on the enormity of their sin. His charitable approach was also signalled by his use here of the term 'brothers'.

Having spoken gently of their personal involvement, Peter immediately pointed his hearers again to what God had done. God had foretold in prophecy that the Messiah would suffer. Jesus had been appointed Messiah for them, and in fulfilment of God's purposes had died for them. Now Jesus had gone to glory and would not return until he came to make all things new.

In the meantime, God was calling them to repent of their sin. Repentance would be followed by remission. That is, if they turned to God in confessing their sin, God would send their sin away into oblivion but would receive them into the fullness of his love.

Throughout his preaching, Peter moved back and fore between the need of his hearers and the fact that everything they needed was to be found in the salvation which God had provided in Jesus.

Now, coming to the application of his message, he reminded his hearers of a famous passage in Deuteronomy chapter 18. In this passage Moses had prophesied that, as he himself had been raised up from among the people, God would yet raise up another prophet like him to whom they would have to listen. If the people of Israel did not listen to that prophet, they would be cut off from the community of God. 'Yes,' said Peter, as he felt the full weight of Old

Testament witness behind him, 'and that is what the testimony of all the prophets amounts to – they were all pointing forward to the times of blessing which the Messiah would bring. You people in Jerusalem are familiar with these Old Testament promises. You know the promise which God made to your father Abraham. He promised that the whole earth would be blessed through his seed. Well, the seed of Abraham has been born, and his name is Jesus. The servant of the Lord has come. You rejected him when he first came to you, but now God is sending him to you again. He has raised him from the dead and he has sent him to bless you today.'

Peter's hearers were used to the Law, and had a strong bent towards legalism. They were not used to thinking of the mercy of God. Peter did his utmost to point them away from what they had done to what God had done – away from their sin to God's grace.

C. H. Spurgeon tells about a minister who went to the house of a poor woman to give her a gift of money. He knocked at the door, but got no answer. He had to come away with the money still in his pocket. Later, he met this lady and told her that he had been at her door. 'When did you call?' she asked. When he told her, she said, 'Oh dear, I heard you, and I am so sorry I did not answer. I thought it was the man calling for the rent.'[9] We think of God as that woman thought of her visitor. But God has not come to our door to collect debts. He has come to give us what will cancel out our debts.

This was the message which Peter sought to drive home to the heart of every one who gathered that day in Solomon's Colonnade.

Pray about it:

1. Peter was concerned to divert the eyes of the crowd from himself and John to the God who had sent his Son to be the source of all blessing in the world. Pray that the church today would not draw attention to herself, but would effectively point people away from herself to her God and her Saviour.

2. Faith means receiving the revelation of himself which God has given in his word, and receiving the Saviour to whom that revelation points.

Stacy O' Connor was brought up to attend the Roman Catholic Church in the U.S.A., but Jesus did not feature prominently in her life. Partly through the loving testimony of a colleague, she came to read the Bible for herself. As she read she asked herself, 'Well, what are you waiting for – an engraved invitation? This is as close as you are going to get!' She knelt down and prayed. 'I acknowledged my sins and thanked God for sending his only Son for my salvation and I asked God to take control of my life. As the tears rolled down my face, I felt the kind of relief you feel when you finally do something you've put off for a long, long time.'[10]

Pray that, through the witness of the church today, many will respond in faith as Stacy O'Connor did.

12. Arrested!

The priests and the captain of the temple guard and the Sadducees came up to Peter and John while they were speaking to the people. They were greatly disturbed because the apostles were teaching the people and proclaiming in Jesus the resurrection of the dead. They seized Peter and John, and because it was evening, they put them in jail until the next day. But many who heard the message believed, and the number of men grew to about five thousand (Acts 4:1-4).

The temple had priests whose function it was to act as guards, or as policemen. It was these men who appeared in the Garden of Gethsemane, armed with clubs, to carry out Jesus' arrest (Luke 22:52).

These temple police became alarmed as Peter preached in Solomon's Colonnade, and went off to report what was happening. Their chief came back with them, and representatives of the Sadducees.

The Sadducees regarded the first five books of Moses as having greater authority than the rest of the Old Testament. They rejected the wealth of oral tradition which was so important to the Pharisees. They did not believe in the resurrection, in the existence of angels or spirits, or in an after life (Acts 23:8). No wonder that they reacted to Peter's preaching about the resurrection of Jesus!

It was too late in the day to call a meeting of the Sanhedrin, so Peter and John were put in a cell for the night.

However, it was also too late to stop the spread of the gospel! On the Day of Pentecost, the number of new believers rose by three thousand. Now Luke says that the number of men in the church in Jerusalem was about five thousand. There would have been women and children too.

Think about it:

The Sadducees probably regarded themselves as intellectually superior, standing above the average believer, whom they dismissed as unthinking and superstitious.

Yet, when in dispute with Jesus about the resurrection, their own limitations were exposed: 'You are mistaken, not knowing the Scriptures nor the power of God' (Matthew 22:29).

13. Not You, but the Spirit Speaking

The next day the rulers, elders and teachers of the law met in Jerusalem. Annas the high priest was there, and so were Caiaphas, John, Alexander and the other men of the high priest's family. They had Peter and John brought before them and began to question them: 'By what power or what name did you do this?' Then Peter, filled with the Holy Spirit, said to them: 'Rulers and elders of the people! If we are being called to account today for an act of kindness shown to a cripple and are asked how he was healed, then know this, you and all the people of Israel: It is by the name of Jesus Christ of Nazareth, whom you crucified but whom God raised from the dead, that this man stands before you healed. He is "the stone you builders rejected, which has become the capstone." Salvation is found in no one else, for there is no other name under heaven given to men by which we must be saved' (Acts 4:5-12).

The Sanhedrin

The Sanhedrin was the highest court among the Jews. Because Israel was a theocracy, owning God as its king, the Sanhedrin was both a civil and an ecclesiastical court. It was made up of three sections.

The 'rulers' were the priestly families who, with their associates, held the positions of greatest influence in the church and in the running of the temple. Luke refers to Annas the High Priest. In his Gospel, he speaks of Annas and Caiaphas as being High Priests. Annas was High Priest from AD 6-15. Caiaphas, who was Annas' son in law, was High Priest from AD 18-36. Probably popular opinion regarded Annas as still being High Priest after AD 15, because his tenure of the office had been ended by the

Romans. The Jews would have regarded the Romans as having no right to depose him.

The 'scribes' were professional interpreters and teachers of the Old Testament law. The 'elders' were lay members. It seems that the rulers were mostly Sadducees (see page 57), the Scribes were mostly Pharisees (see page 89), and the elders also followed the teaching of the Pharisees.

The Sanhedrin had seventy members, plus the High Priest who acted as President. They sat in a raised part of the Court Room, arranged in a semi-circle.

A Spirit-filled testimony

The question concerning the court was – 'In connection with which name, or on the basis of what authority, did you heal this cripple?'

Peter could have been filled with fear of these men, but instead he was filled with the Spirit of God. His experience was exactly as Jesus had promised: 'On my account you will be brought before governors and kings as a witness to them and to the Gentiles. But when they arrest you, do not worry about what to say or how to say it. At that time you will be given what to say, *for it will not be you speaking, but the Spirit of your Father speaking through you*' (Matthew 10:18-20).

Because of being filled with the Spirit, Peter was now like a different man from the coward who had been so frightened as to deny Jesus on the night of his arrest. He spoke to the Sanhedrin with poise and power.

With perhaps a touch of humour, he suggested that the court should be investigating acts of wickedness – not good deeds such as he and John had done! Then he explained that the power of the risen Christ held the key to the healing of the cripple. He and John were only the channels through whom that power had flowed.

That brought him on to the real issue before the court. Jesus, the author of this miracle, was the one against whom this very court had set itself. They, the master builders of Israel, seeking a solid basis on which the church and state could rest, had rejected Jesus. But God had raised him from the dead! (Peter could never lose any chance to set in the starkest contrast the verdict of mere men and the unanswerable judgment of God regarding Jesus.)

Now nothing could stop Peter from proclaiming that salvation which is in Christ and in no one else. The cripple had felt the healing which flows from Jesus. Every member of the Sanhedrin must also experience to the full that healing for himself, or else be lost.

Think about it:
The reason why Peter avoided the mistakes made by the Sadducees was that he was guided by the very things which they ignored – the word and power of God (Matthew 22:29, see page 58).

Pray about it:
Every person who is joined to Jesus in living faith has been baptised by the Spirit (1 Corinthians 12:13). Yet, as Paul says in Ephesians 5:18, we are in constant need that the Spirit would flow through us in a fresh way. This fresh infilling with the Spirit was what Peter experienced, in fulfilment of Jesus' promise in Matthew 10:20.

Pray that every member of the body of Christ would experience that filling with his Spirit today.

14. They Had Been With Jesus

When they saw the courage of Peter and John and realized that they were unschooled, ordinary men, they were astonished and they took note that these men had been with Jesus. But since they could see the man who had been healed standing there with them, there was nothing they could say. So they ordered them to withdraw from the Sanhedrin and then conferred together. 'What are we going to do with these men?' they asked. 'Everybody living in Jerusalem knows they have done an outstanding miracle, and we cannot deny it. But to stop this thing from spreading any further among the people, we must warn these men to speak no longer to anyone in this name' (Acts 4:13-17).

The shadow of Jesus

As the case went on, two things became clear.

Firstly, Peter was speaking with the ease of someone who had been pleading in law courts all his life. But neither he nor John had had any legal training or experience whatever. They were just working men from Galilee, as even their accents confirmed.

Then the members of the Sanhedrin began to think of Jesus. It was not so long since he had appeared before this court. He, too, had lacked formal training. Yet he, too, had confounded the religious experts by his knowledge and his authority. At last, the full realisation dawned. The men before the court that morning had been with Jesus! As these unlearned men from Galilee spoke with unanswerable authority, the shadow of Jesus himself settled once more over the court.

At that point they put Peter and John out so that they could throw together, in their growing desperation, whatever ideas they could produce.

'What can we do?'

'Well, for a start, the cripple beggar has been healed by these men. Everyone in Jerusalem knows that. Even those who have come to Jerusalem from abroad will have seen him at the Beautiful Gate. Jews from the far corners of the Roman Empire will know that he has been healed. He is within these precincts as we speak, showing to all the world that he has been healed, and we cannot deny it.'

(One response to the situation does not seem to have occurred to them – that they should repent of their rejection of Jesus and seek God's forgiveness. Sometimes the most obvious solution is the most difficult to see.)

Its hands were tied

Then they called them in again and commanded them not to speak or teach at all in the name of Jesus. But Peter and John replied, 'Judge for yourselves whether it is right in God's sight to obey you rather than God. For we cannot help speaking about what we have seen and heard.' After further threats they let them go. They could not decide how to punish them, because all the people were praising God for what had happened. For the man who was miraculously healed was over forty years old (Acts 4:18-22).

In the end, the court went for damage limitation. They called in Peter and John, and warned them not to speak again in the name of Jesus. Perhaps, in that way, this cancerous interest in Jesus would stop spreading through the Jewish world.

When Peter heard the court's ban on the use of Jesus'

name, he did not lose his poise for a moment. He told the court that it could come to whatever decision it wished, though it would have to answer for its decision to a higher authority. He then stated frankly that neither he nor John could comply with the court's instructions. They had met the risen Christ. They had been called by the highest authority of all to witness to the world that God had raised Jesus from the dead. It would no more be possible for them to choke back their testimony to the risen Christ than it would be possible to push the steam back down the spout of a kettle that was sitting on top of a roaring fire.

The Sanhedrin was not used to being addressed like that. Some outraged members spoke of punishing these prisoners for contempt of court. But the shouts of the crowd outside filled the air. It seemed that all Jerusalem was being swept along on a wave of enthusiasm for this upstart from Nazareth. Perhaps, another day, the authority of the Sanhedrin would be vindicated. But, for today, its hands were tied.

Think about it:
The Sanhedrin had the power and the prestige. The apostles had no power and no prestige. Yet the members of the Sanhedrin were perplexed, afraid, and in the end helpless; while the witness of the apostles was fearless and effective.

One difference was that the Sanhedrin, for all its talk about God, was taken up with its own authority, its own self-image – whereas the apostles, free from such bondage to themselves, were concerned only to know and to do the will of God.

Pray about it:

There was a factor which vitally affected events in the court that day, though it was hidden from the eyes of the Sanhedrin members. It was the presence and power of the Holy Spirit. He who was present in the ministry of Jesus was present also with the apostles, lending his weight to their testimony.

Pray that the church today will be filled with the Spirit, as Peter was. Then the power of Jesus will be felt again in the world, as the church testifies to him.

15. Lord, Consider Their Threats

More pressure, more prayer

On their release, Peter and John went back to their own people and reported all that the chief priests and elders had said to them. When they heard this, they raised their voices together in prayer to God. 'Sovereign Lord,' they said, 'you made the heaven and the earth and the sea, and everything in them. You spoke by the Holy Spirit through the mouth of your servant, our father David: "Why do the nations rage and the peoples plot in vain? The kings of the earth take their stand and the rulers gather together against the Lord and against his Anointed One." Indeed Herod and Pontius Pilate met together with the Gentiles and the people of Israel in this city to conspire against your holy servant Jesus, whom you anointed. They did what your power and will had decided beforehand should happen' (Acts 4:23-28).

Leaving the Sanhedrin Peter and John made their way to the more congenial company of their fellow believers, and told how the court had placed a ban on any attempt to spread the gospel of Christ. The opposition to the church, pressing in on the horizontal plane from their fellow men, caused the church to reach up unitedly on the vertical plane to God.

It was the same in Old Testament times, in the days of Hezekiah. The Assyrians pressed in on the little kingdom of Judah, threatening to destroy it. But this pressure had the effect of fusing the hearts of the king and the prophet, Isaiah, so that they united in calling on the help of God (Isaiah 37:1,2,6). And this is not the only parallel between the situation of the New Testament church in Acts 4 and the Old Testament church in Isaiah 37.

In both situations, the church took hold in prayer of the biblical teaching that God is Lord of all – ruling at the creation of the world, and ruling in the present; sovereign over the details of the church's circumstances, and sovereign over the church's enemies. Hezekiah said, 'O Lord Almighty, God of Israel ... you alone are God over all the kingdoms of the earth. You have made heaven and earth.' The early church said, 'Sovereign Lord, you made the heaven and the earth and the sea, and everything in them.'

The apostles went on to quote Psalm 2, in which God's enemies are pictured as drawing themselves up in opposition to him. There is such a build-up of their forces, and their opposition is so fierce. But all this massive build-up leads to – *nothing!* The early church saw a vivid and precise fulfilment of these words in Jesus' death. The nations, represented by the Romans, combined with the people of Israel to secure the crucifixion of the Son of God. In this they were assisted by Herod and Pilate. (Luke tells us in chapter 23:11-12 of his Gospel that Herod and Pilate, who previously had been at loggerheads, buried their differences in making common cause against Jesus.) But what was accomplished by this impressive display of unity among the forces of evil? Precisely 'what your power and will had decided beforehand should happen'!

The apostles then prayed for three things. First, they asked God simply to 'consider their threats'. Hezekiah showed exactly the same spirit. When he had received the threatening letter from his enemies, he 'went up to the temple of the Lord, and spread it out before the Lord.' Second, the apostles prayed for boldness. They did not pray for their safety. In fact, what they did pray for was likely to lead them into further danger, as it would involve them in open disobedience to the Sanhedrin. Third, the apostles prayed for further displays of God's miraculous power, backing up their preaching of his gospel.

More prayer, more power

'Now, Lord, consider their threats and enable your servants to speak your word with great boldness. Stretch out your hand to heal and perform miraculous signs and wonders through the name of your holy servant Jesus.' After they prayed, the place where they were meeting was shaken. And they were all filled with the Holy Spirit and spoke the word of God boldly (Acts 4:29-31).

The answer came quickly and dramatically. First, the place where the church was gathered was shaken. Second, they were all filled with the Holy Spirit. Third, this fresh infilling with the Spirit evidenced itself in the boldness with which believers made known the word of God.

How weak the decree which demanded their silence, and how powerful the presence of God which constrained them to speak!

Think about it:

1. Neither Hezekiah nor the apostles wasted time in speaking, either among themselves or to others, against their oppressors. All their time and nervous energy were spent in prayer to God. How much do we follow their example, when others oppose what we do for God?

2. Never was the sovereignty of God displayed more majestically than when evil forces within and outwith the church combined to secure the crucifixion of the Son of

God. Out of what men did in their wickedness came the victory which God had previously planned in his grace.

Pray about it:
1. We are often bound in our prayers because we are so concerned about our own interests. Pray that you would be free from a self-centred spirit, as the apostles were.

2. The place was shaken when the Old Testament church was set up at Sinai, and when the New Testament church was set up in Jerusalem. Pray that, in so far as this may be necessary, the church would be shaken up again today.

3. Tolerance of everything and anything seems to be regarded today as the most outstanding virtue of all. It has become almost a religion in itself. The early believers had an uncompromising boldness, deriving from the fulness of the Spirit in their hearts. Pray that the church today would have that boldness which the early believers had, making known without compromise the gospel of Christ.

16. What Life Was Like

> All the believers were one in heart and mind. No one
> claimed that any of his possessions was his own, but they
> shared everything they had. With great power the apostles
> continued to testify to the resurrection of the Lord Jesus,
> and much grace was upon them all. There were no needy
> persons among them. For from time to time those who
> owned lands or houses sold them, brought the money from
> the sales and put it at the apostles' feet, and it was
> distributed to anyone as he had need (Acts 4:32-35).

After telling about the descent of the Spirit on the Day of
Pentecost, Luke described the church which had been
transformed by the Spirit's power (2:42-47). Now that the
church had received a fresh in-filling with the Spirit, Luke
gives us another picture of what life in the church was like.

There was a unity of spirit. Because believers united in
loving God with all their heart and soul, they were united to
one another. The fruit of the Spirit is love.

This love showed itself in practical ways. Some say that
the situation in the early church represents a form of com-
munism, with the abolition of the right to private property.
That right was abolished among the Essene community at
Qumran, on the north west corner of the Dead Sea. But that
it was not abolished in the early church we see for example
from Acts 12:12 where we are told that, after his release
from prison, Peter made his way to a house which is still
described as belonging to Mary, the mother of John Mark.
What came as a fruit of the Spirit was, a change of attitude
towards the property which believers had. The natural
tendency to say 'That belongs to me' receded. In its place
came a powerful sense that the church was one body, and a

deep sensitivity to the needs of other members of that body. This meant that, whenever a case of need arose in the church, there were others within the church who would respond to that need. They would sell something of value, give the proceeds to the church, and the church would direct this help towards the believer who was in need. Not one member of the church was left to lack the necessities of life.

The second evidence of the Spirit's presence with the church was, the power which accompanied the apostles' testimony to Jesus' resurrection from the dead.

The third change which the Spirit made when he came was, to cause 'much grace' to rest on believers. (This was no doubt connected with the powerful, Spirit-filled preaching of the apostles. Preaching is intended to be a means by which hearers taste for themselves the grace of God.) This grace made the church attractive to those outside (Acts 2:47).

Pray about it:
Pray for these three signs of the Spirit's work within the church today:

1. Unity of heart, crossing denominational boundaries, and showing itself in practical ways.

2. Powerful preaching of the gospel.

3. The grace of God resting on the whole church, transforming the hearts and lives of believers and making them attractive to those outside the church.

17. Two Cases in Contrast

Joseph, a Levite from Cyprus, whom the apostles called Barnabas (which means Son of Encouragement), sold a field he owned and brought the money and put it at the apostles' feet. Now a man named Ananias, together with his wife Sapphira, also sold a piece of property. With his wife's full knowledge he kept back part of the money for himself, but brought the rest and put it at the apostles' feet. Then Peter said, 'Ananias, how is it that Satan has so filled your heart that you have lied to the Holy Spirit and have kept for yourself some of the money you received for the land? Didn't it belong to you before it was sold? And after it was sold, wasn't the money at your disposal? What made you think of doing such a thing? You have not lied to men but to God.' When Ananias heard this, he fell down and died. And great fear seized all who heard what had happened. Then the young men came forward, wrapped up his body, and carried him out and buried him. About three hours later his wife came in, not knowing what had happened. Peter asked her, 'Tell me, is this the price you and Ananias got for the land?' 'Yes,' she said, 'that is the price.' Peter said to her, 'How could you agree to test the Spirit of the Lord? Look! The feet of the men who buried your husband are at the door, and they will carry you out also.' At that moment she fell down at his feet and died. Then the young men came in and, finding her dead, carried her out and buried her beside her husband (Acts 4:36-5:10).

Barnabas

What Luke describes was not a single event, but an ongoing process. It was not once but many times that a need arose within the fellowship and someone realised the value of an asset and brought the proceeds of the sale to the apostles so that the money could go to the person in need. Then Luke gives us an example.

Barnabas was a Jew belonging to Cyprus. He had relatives in Jerusalem, and he seems to have owned a field there too. In response to the need of others in the church Barnabas sold the field, brought the proceeds, and laid them at the apostles' feet.

Ananias and Sapphira

Having given us an example of genuine generosity Luke then gives us a contrasting example, which was marred by hypocrisy.

Ananias and Sapphira also possessed a piece of land. They also brought money from the sale of this land and placed it at the apostles' feet. On the surface, it seemed as if they had acted precisely as Barnabas had done.

Actually, Ananias and Sapphira had acted more like Achan than like Barnabas. Achan's story is told in Joshua, chapter 7.

Before the Children of Israel entered Jericho, Joshua had warned them that all the silver and the gold of the city was to be consecrated to the Lord (Joshua 6:19). But Achan, seeing some of the wealth of the city, coveted it and took it for himself (Joshua 7:21). The sin of Achan had immediate and far-reaching implications for the whole church. The Children of Israel were poised to possess the promised land. But, instead of this, their progress was arrested and they were defeated by their enemies. God showed Joshua that there was no way forward until Israel had been purged of this sin.

The church was poised for rapid progress, too, in the time of Ananias and Sapphira. It was the time when many Old

Testament promises were about to be fulfilled, when the church was about to possess the spiritual ground previously occupied by the heathen. But, again, the sin of individuals had to be exposed and judged before the church as a body could move on.

The Holy Spirit was there

We cannot tell precisely what the motive for this deception was. Perhaps Ananias coveted a place of honour, and even of power, in the church. In any case, he and his wife agreed that they would sell their property and pretend to give the whole of the proceeds to God, while in reality they kept back part of the price. At the appropriate point during a time of worship, Ananias came forward and presented his offering. But the Holy Spirit was there. That was the outstanding feature of life in the early church. The presence of the Holy Spirit was a powerful, inescapable reality. The Holy Spirit made Peter aware in some way of the deception which was being carried out in the church that day. Peter's brief conversation with this New Testament Achan highlights four things.

(i) It confirms the fact that there was no abrogation of private property in the early church. There was no law forcing Ananias to part with his property. He was free to dispose of it as he saw fit.

(ii) It shows that the early church had a profound awareness of the fact that it was the Holy Spirit (rather, for example, than the apostles) who was himself conducting the affairs of the church. Peter charges Ananias with lying, not to himself but to the Holy Spirit.

(iii) Although the Holy Spirit was such a powerful presence in the church, Satan was there too. By conspiring with his wife to perpetrate a deception in the immediate presence of the Holy Spirit Ananias had, at least in this particular issue, yielded himself to the influence of the arch enemy of the church and of God. No church is perfect.

(iv) Peter's question brought home Ananias' individual responsibility – *Why did you do it, Ananias?* Whether or not the shock of having his deception unveiled in front of the church triggered a physical reaction like a heart attack, Ananias collapsed at once and died.

An opportunity to repent

Three hours later his wife Sapphira came into this gathering for worship. Peter knew that she and her husband had agreed to commit this sin. He gave her an opportunity to repent, but she did not take it. So the fate which had befallen her husband befell her also.

These evidences of the Spirit's working in the daily life of the church had a profound impact, both within the church and beyond.

Think about it:

1. Contrary to what Jehovah's Witnesses and others say, the Holy Spirit is not merely an influence. You do not lie to an influence, but to a person. In any case Peter expressly stated that, in lying to the Holy Spirit, Ananias and Sapphira had lied to God.

2. Barnabas and others in Jerusalem could have thought of many reasons why they should not part with their property. Perhaps, when times would change, they would need all their assets to support themselves. (We learn from 1 Corinthians 9:6 that, at a later stage, Barnabas did have to work to support himself. Also, the church in Jerusalem

came on hard times and had to be relieved by the generosity
of Christians from outside Palestine.) However, if we wait
till we are certain that there is no risk whatever involved, we
will never do anything at all for God.'Whoever watches the
wind will not plant; whoever looks at the clouds will not
reap' (Ecclesiastes 11:4).

Pray about it:
1. Although the incident of Ananias and Sapphira involved
drastic action for the exposure of sin in the church, it was
good for believers to be reminded that they served a holy
God. Pray that this awareness will fill the modern church
too.

2. Ananias and Sapphira exposed themselves to the
influence of Satan. The best protection against this is being
constantly filled with the Holy Spirit. Pray that each believer will be filled with the Spirit in heart and life, and that
Satan will thus be prevented from gaining a foothold in the
church.

3. Barnabas, whose name may mean 'son of soothing',
was used to cement bonds between believers in the early
church. When the leaders of the Jerusalem church were
suspicious of the newly converted Saul of Tarsus, it was
Barnabas who persuaded them to accept him (Acts 9:26-
27). When Jews who had a Gentile background began to be
converted, and there was a danger that the leaders of the
church in Jerusalem would not receive them, Barnabas went
north and encouraged these new believers (Acts 11:22-24).
Such was the ministry of a man who was 'full of the Holy
Spirit, and of faith' (Acts 11:24). Pray that you will be like
Barnabas – or like St. Francis, whose famous prayer expresses the Spirit in which Barnabas lived:

Lord, make me an instrument of your peace.
Where there is hatred, may I bring love;
Where there is injury, pardon;
Where there is discord, unity;
Where there is doubt, faith;
Where there is despair, hope;
Where there is sadness, joy;
Where there is darkness, light.

Master, grant that I may not so much seek
*   to be consoled, as to console;*
*   to be understood, as to understand;*
*   to be loved, as to love.*

For it is in giving that we receive.
It is in pardoning that we are pardoned.
It is in dying that we rise again to eternal life.

18. Another Picture of the Early Church

Great fear seized the whole church and all who heard about these events. The apostles performed many miraculous signs and wonders among the people. And all the believers used to meet together in Solomon's Colonnade. No one else dared join them, even though they were highly regarded by the people. Nevertheless, more and more men and women believed in the Lord and were added to their number. As a result, people brought the sick into the streets and laid them on beds and mats so that at least Peter's shadow might fall on some of them as he passed by. Crowds gathered also from the towns around Jerusalem, bringing their sick and those tormented by evil spirits, and all of them were healed (Acts 5:11-16).

Luke has already given us two pictures of the growing New Testament church: in chapter 2:41-47, and in chapter 4:32-37. Here again, after some dramatic developments, he wants us to see and feel what life was like in the early church.

Fear
The Bible tells us (e.g., in I John 4:18) that fear is the result of sin, and that where the gospel takes effect we are delivered from bondage to fear. But Luke also tells us that the death of Ananias and Sapphira had the effect of making people feel afraid. This makes us think of a verse like Proverbs 3:7: 'Fear the LORD and shun evil.' There is nothing wrong with fear in the form of not wanting to grieve God. These people had such an overwhelming sense of the greatness and glory of God that all they wanted to do was to please him.

Signs

After hearing the decision of the Sanhedrin, banning them from preaching in the name of Jesus, the apostles had unitedly prayed that God would vindicate his word by accompanying the preaching of the gospel with signs of his healing power (4:30). After the church had been purged of the sin connected with Ananias and Sapphira, the power of God flowed through the apostles in even greater measure than before. There had been one sign of his holiness when the purifying fire of God's judgment had burned to the heart of the life of the church. Now there were many signs of his mercy and grace, as the healing power of God reached out through the hands of the apostles to many who suffered throughout Jerusalem.

Worship

They had been banned from preaching anywhere, yet the apostles held meetings within the temple precincts – the area over which those banning them had special jurisdiction. Their prayers for boldness (4:29) were being answered! Despite the ban of the Sanhedrin, the believers met in Solomon's Colonnade, which for the time being they seem to have made almost their own.

The others who frequented the temple area seem to have given them a wide berth. They did not rush into the crowds of Christians, demanding in a loud voice what was going on. Nor did those who had no understanding of the gospel demand presumptuously to become members of this growing group. The church enjoyed a healthy respect in the eyes of those outside. They knew that something special was going on in Solomon's Colonnade.

Growth

Although no one clamoured to join the church who was
ignorant of Christ, Luke tells us at the same time that crowds
of people joined the church who were true believers. There
were vast numbers, both of men and women. Ananias was
gone from the scene, but multitudes of male believers took
his place. Sapphira was not around any more, but an increasing number of believing women were there instead. Luke
has told us that three thousand were converted on the Day of
Pentecost (2:41). He has reported, at a later date, that the
number of male believers stood at five thousand (4:4). From
now on, however, he abandons all such figures. There were
crowds and crowds – an accurate impression of how remarkable was the rate of growth just could not be conveyed.

More signs

With more people being converted, there was more faith
around. With increased faith, there was greater expectation
of what God could do. People began to drag out the sick and
to lay them down in the streets, so that even the shadow of
him who had been such a channel of God's power to their
city might fall on them.

And so the healing power of God took a deeper hold on
the people of Jerusalem. Even those who were tormented
(literally, *crowded*) by unclean spirits were healed. The
healing went deep, and it went wide. Streams of sick people
began to pour into Jerusalem from the surrounding cities
too.

19. The Sadducees, the Angel, and the Sanhedrin

The Sadducees

> Then the high priest and all his associates, who were members of the party of the Sadducees, were filled with jealousy. They arrested the apostles and put them in the public jail (Acts 5:17-18).

The Sadducees did not believe in the resurrection, nor in the existence of angels, nor spirits (see page 57). It seems that the High Priest, together with the others who exercised a controlling influence within the Sanhedrin, belonged to this group.

Luke has already told us that the Sadducees were angry at Peter's preaching about the resurrection, following on the healing of the cripple beggar (4:1f.). It was that anger which led to the imprisonment of Peter and John. Now the Sadducees were jealous. They were the people with the power, and they were jealous because the apostles were obviously enjoying increasing popular support. Under the leadership of the High Priest, they were stung into action and placed all the apostles under lock and key.

The angel

> But during the night an angel of the Lord opened the doors of the jail and brought them out. 'Go, stand in the temple courts,' he said, 'and tell the people the full message of this new life' (Acts 5:19-20).

But, in the quietness of the night, an angel came and set the prisoners free. Presumably the guards, watching at the prison door, were prevented in some way from observing. Perhaps they were made to sleep with unusual depth as this visitor first unlocked the doors, let the apostles out, then locked the doors again. No evidence was left behind of what had happened. But the fact remained that a being in whose existence the Sadducees did not believe had come and set their prisoners free.

Not only that. He also handed them a message from heaven: 'Go ... tell the people the full message of this new life.' Peter himself had used a phrase like this on a famous occasion. When others had forsaken the ministry of Jesus, and Jesus turned to the disciples to ask if they were going to leave him too, Peter asked bluntly where they could go. Then he added, 'You have the words of eternal life' (John 6:68).

Eugenia Price tells about her conversion in a New York hotel in 1949. She was a sophisticated woman and a successful writer, but there in the presence of a Christian friend she said, 'Oh God, I wish I were dead!' Her friend Ellen said, 'Genie, it would be wonderful if you would die ... if the old Gene Price would die right now – this minute – so the new one can be born.'[11] That hotel room witnessed the death and the rebirth of Eugenia Price. Now she could understand the meaning of the words used by Peter and by the angel when they testified to the unique life-giving power of the gospel of Christ.

The Sanhedrin

At daybreak they entered the temple courts, as they had been told, and began to teach the people. When the high priest and his associates arrived, they called together the Sanhedrin –

the full assembly of the elders of the Israel – and sent to the
jail for the apostles. But on arriving at the jail, the officers did
not find them there. So they went back and reported. 'We
found the jail securely locked, with the guards standing at the
doors; but when we opened them, we found no one inside.'
On hearing this report, the captain of the temple guard and the
chief priests were puzzled, wondering what would come of
this. Then someone came and said, 'Look! The men you put
in jail are standing in the temple courts teaching the people'
(Acts 5:21-25).

In the morning the High Priest and his associates were
hurrying about, organising a full meeting of the Sanhedrin.
Once this was under way, they sent members of the temple
police to bring the apostles round from the prison. They
were in for a shock. The temple police reported to the full
council that they had gone to the prison, had found everything in order, but had found the prison deserted. There was
not a prisoner in sight.

The members of the Sanhedrin were more than perplexed. They knew that the apostles commanded popular
support. It was this support which had kept the Sanhedrin
back from treating the apostles more severely on the previous occasion (4:21). What was going on now? Were there
those, even among themselves, who sympathised with this
new heresy? Was that how the prisoners had escaped?

Then the really shattering news broke. The men who
were supposed to be appearing as prisoners before the
Sanhedrin in one part of the temple area were at that very
moment preaching to crowds of people in another part of the
same precincts!

Think about it:

For matters spiritual and civil, the Sanhedrin had vested in it the full power and authority of the nation of Israel. Yet one angel encouraged the apostles in their belief that ultimate authority and power rested with the God whom they feared, trusted and obeyed, rather than with this earthly court. The Sanhedrin exercised its power by locking the apostles up. The angel set them free. The Sanhedrin banned the preaching of the gospel. But the angel, invoking a superior authority, commanded the apostles to go and preach.

Whatever opposition the church encounters it is called to go forward, trusting to the absolute power and ultimate authority of God. 'If God is for us, who can be against us?' (Romans 8:31).

20. On Trial Again

An echo from the past

> At that, the captain went with his officers and brought the
> apostles. They did not use force, because they feared that the
> people would stone them. Having brought the apostles, they
> made them appear before the Sanhedrin to be questioned by
> the high priest. 'We gave you strict orders not to teach in this
> name,' he said. 'Yet you have filled Jerusalem with your
> teaching and are determined to make us guilty of this man's
> blood' (Acts 5:26-28).

On the previous occasion, the captain of the temple had sent
his underlings to deal with the apostles. This time, he went
himself. He had lost prestige through the escape of the
prisoners. Perhaps he now hoped to drag the apostles before
the Sanhedrin with a show of force fitted to cow the
prisoners and to restore his prestige before the court.

As things worked out, the crowd around the apostles
complained against the captain of the temple for coming to
take the apostles away. There was even some talk of stoning.
Stoning was an act by which something which threatened to
defile the Jewish nation was publicly purged. And it was the
captain of the temple whom the people were speaking of
stoning! Support for the apostles at this point was reaching
fever pitch. But, despite public support which the apostles
could have exploited to create a riot, they came quietly
round with the captain of the temple from where they had
been preaching to where the Sanhedrin was sitting.

When the apostles had been set in front of the court, the
High Priest addressed them in a blustering way. He did not
ask about how they had succeeded in escaping from prison.

As a Sadducee, he did not believe in angels. It would not have appealed to him to be told that it was an angel who had just set his prisoners free! The only thing in the mind of the High Priest was the fact that the court had issued a ban on preaching in the name of Jesus, and that the apostles had had the nerve to disobey that ban. (He was so upset by what they had done that he could not bring himself to mention the name of Jesus but could only say with contempt *this name*).

In the strength of God's Spirit

> Peter and the other apostles replied: 'We must obey God rather than men! The God of our fathers raised Jesus from the dead – whom you had killed by hanging him on a tree. God exalted him to his own right hand as Prince and Saviour that he might give repentance and forgiveness of sins to Israel. We are witnesses of these things and so is the Holy Spirit, whom God has given to those who obey him' (Acts 5:29-32).

Peter was not in the least intimidated by the High Priest. His statement, 'We must obey God rather than men!' is similar to that given during his previous appearance (4:19-20); but the thought is expressed more forcefully. In the interval, he had had his calling to speak about Jesus confirmed directly by an angel.

Now, in the strength of God's Spirit, Peter turned towards the members of the court to make an outspoken accusation. 'You murdered the Son of God,' he said. 'You even marked him as one accursed by God.' (The Jews did not crucify, but they hanged the bodies of criminals on a tree after execution as a sign that they were cursed of God. Peter was saying that, in securing the crucifixion of Jesus by the hands of the Romans, the Jews were consciously aiming to proclaim that Jesus had died under the divine curse.) 'However,' Peter went on, 'he whom you put down into the gutter God has raised to the highest heaven.' Then Peter preached to them the gospel of the grace of God. He told these guilty men that Jesus, rather than employ his absolute authority to destroy them, would use it 'to give repentance and forgiveness of sins to Israel'.

Peter finished by saying emphatically that this gospel was not something which he and the other apostles had dreamed up. They were simply testifying to what God had done and said. In fact it was the Holy Spirit himself who, at that moment, was testifying through them to what God had done.

Think about it:
The High Priest said that the apostles, in the short time since the resurrection of Jesus, had filled Jerusalem with the gospel. He meant this as an accusation, whereas it was actually an unintended compliment. If we were in the apostles' situation, would we merit such an 'accusation'?

Pray about it:
In John 15:26-27 Jesus promises his disciples, 'When the Counsellor comes, whom I will send to you from the Father, the Spirit of truth who goes out from the Father, he will testify about me. And you also must testify...'.

Pray that your heart and life will be surrendered to the influence of this Helper from heaven, as those of the apostles were. Then, when you witness, it will not so much be you who witnesses as the Holy Spirit who witnesses through you.

21. Help from an Unexpected Quarter

When they heard this, they were furious and wanted to put them to death. But a Pharisee named Gamaliel, a teacher of the law, who was honoured by all the people, stood up in the Sanhedrin and ordered that the men be put outside for a little while. Then he addressed them: 'Men of Israel, consider carefully what you intend to do to these men. Some time ago Theudas appeared, claiming to be somebody, and about four hundred men rallied to him. He was killed, all his followers were dispersed, and it all came to nothing. After him, Judas the Galilean appeared in the days of the census and led a band of people in revolt. He too was killed, and all his followers were scattered. Therefore, in the present case I advise you: Leave these men alone! Let them go! For if their purpose or activity is of human origin, it will fail. But if it is from God, you will not be able to stop these men; you will only find yourselves fighting against God' (Acts 5:33-42).

When Peter accused his hearers on the Day of Pentecost of murdering God's Son, they were convicted of their sin. Now that he repeated the charge before the Sanhedrin, the effect was different. Instead of being broken and contrite, the members of the Sanhedrin were incensed.

Gamaliel

At this point, Luke introduces us to Gamaliel. His grandfather Hillel was famous, not only for his vast learning, but also for the moderation with which he applied the principles of rabbinical teaching to the cases which were brought to him. Gamaliel himself became famous in his own right as a rabbi, but also as the teacher of Saul of Tarsus (Acts 22:3).

Gamaliel's contribution to this crucial debate in the

Sanhedrin reflects a moderation which he may have learned from his grandfather. More importantly, it shows that God could summon help from an unexpected quarter for the protection of his infant church.

The Pharisees

It is also at this point that Luke introduces the Pharisees. This was the party, in the Jewish church and in the Sanhedrin, to which Gamaliel belonged.

The term 'pharisee' means separated. Pharisees regarded themselves as standing apart from others who did not keep the law of God as they did. This law of God, to which they devoted themselves, was not simply the Scriptures as given to the church through Moses. It also included a mass of detailed legislation which, it was claimed, had been handed down from Moses by word of mouth.

The Pharisees were obsessed with observing faithfully every little detail of these rules and regulations. However, because of their overwhelming concern to follow an outward form, the more basic call to love God and their neighbour was largely ignored.

(The followers of the Pharisees greatly outnumbered those of the Sadducees throughout the Jewish nation. Within the Sanhedrin, too, the majority of members seem to have been Pharisees. However, because of their better connections and their greater political astuteness, the Sadducees seem to have exercised a controlling influence in the Sanhedrin.)

Gamaliel's intervention

At this crucial stage in the debate on how to handle the growing Christian church, Gamaliel intervened. As a Pharisee, he did not belong to the party which generally got its way in the Sanhedrin. But because Gamaliel commanded enormous respect throughout the nation, the Sanhedrin listened to what he had to say.

Gamaliel began with a general warning against the prevailing excitement, the clamour to do something decisive. He then gave two examples of individuals who had made great claims for themselves, who had succeeded in attracting followers, but who had soon disappeared from the scene. Lastly he said that, if this movement connected with Jesus was of God it would be impossible to stop it, whatever the Sanhedrin thought or did.

Gamaliel's intervention proved decisive. His words had sufficient weight to put an end for the time being to plans for killing the apostles. The Sanhedrin did subject them to a savage beating, to reinforce a renewed ban on preaching in the name of Jesus, but then they let the prisoners go.

The ban had no effect whatever. In private houses, and in the temple area, the apostles continued to proclaim the good news that Jesus is the Christ. In fact they did so with a fresh anointing of God's Spirit. As to their shameful mistreatment by the Sanhedrin, the apostles positively rejoiced at the privilege of suffering for the sake of their Lord.

Think about it:
The Sanhedrin was divided between the Sadducees and the Pharisees. (Luke mentions this in chapter 23, where he tells us that Paul made use of this division while addressing the court.)

Although Luke does not spell this out, the fact that the Sadducean leaders of the Sanhedrin wanted to have the apostles killed would have predisposed their rivals the

Pharisees to adopt an opposite, more moderate line. This was the line which Gamaliel took up.

At this crucial moment in the development of the early church God evidently used this prominent Pharisee, together with the division between his party and the Sadducees, to protect his church. How often God uses men over whom the church has no influence, and situations over which they have no control, to protect them in fulfilment of his promises and in answer to their prayers! How heartily the church will sing, looking back from the end of time over all such situations, 'Hallelujah! For our Lord God Almighty reigns' (Revelation 19:6).

22. Growing Pains

The problem

> In those days when the number of disciples was increasing,
> the Grecian Jews among them complained against the
> Hebraic Jews because their widows were being overlooked
> in the daily distribution of food (Acts 6:1).

Luke is developing his account of the early church towards
the point where the church is going to expand into areas
outside Palestine. Playing a significant role in this expansion will be the Greek-speaking members of the church.
Antioch also will play a central role in this expansion. In this
section, Luke introduces us both to the Greek-speaking
converts and to Antioch.

Most of the Greek-speaking Jews lived outside Palestine. They were aware of Greek customs and culture. They
met in synagogues where the Septuagint (the Greek transla-
tion of the Hebrew Old Testament) was read. There was
some tension between them and the Jews who were born and
brought up in Palestine. It seems that, when Greek-speaking
Jews were converted and came into the early church, some
of the tension which existed between the two groups in the
Jewish world was imported into the Christian church. Representatives of the two groups met in the Jerusalem church
because, although most Grecian Jews lived outside Palestine, some had returned to their homeland.

Money was coming into the church from the sale of
property. This money was being handled by the apostles for
the relief of distress among the poor in the church. However,
with the number of converts growing, it was increasingly

difficult for the apostles to ensure that the resources available were being distributed with absolute fairness. This was the practical issue which brought to the surface the tension between the Palestinian and the Grecian Jews in the Jerusalem church. The Grecian Jews complained that those in need among them were being neglected in favour of those in need among Palestinian Jews.

The problem addressed

So the Twelve gathered all the disciples together and said, 'It would not be right for us to neglect the ministry of the word of God in order to wait on tables. Brothers, choose seven men from among you who are known to be full of the Spirit and wisdom. We will turn this responsibility over to them and will give our attention to prayer and the ministry of the word.' This proposal pleased the whole group. They chose Stephen, a man full of faith and of the Holy Spirit; also Philip, Procorus, Nicanor, Timon, Parmenas, and Nicolas from Antioch, a convert to Judaism. They presented these men to the apostles, who prayed and laid their hands on them (Acts 6:2-6).

The apostles called the church together to face this problem at once. They did not prescribe exactly what should be done, but they advised that the church should chose seven men to deal with the problem. The apostles only laid down that these should be men whose reputations were above suspicion, who were wise, and who were filled with the Holy Spirit.

This proposal gained acceptance among both camps in the church, and seven men were duly elected. Stephen is the first name on the list. A man full of faith and of the Holy Spirit, he was to shine as a defender of the faith. Philip was to excel as an evangelist. The church needs both.

The last man on the list is the only one for whom Luke supplied his place of origin. He is Nicolas, born a pagan and coming from Antioch in the north. Luke had a particular reason to slip in this reference to Antioch. He was soon to feature this Syrian city as the base from which the early missionary activity of the church would be launched.

When the process of election had been completed these seven stood before the apostles, who laid their hands on them and prayed. It was a gesture which signified two things. First of all, the apostles assured the seven that the ministry which they were beginning was one in which they had the support of the apostles and of the whole church. Secondly, having been elected and set apart, the responsibility for administering this project was now firmly placed on the shoulders of these seven men.

Further growth

> So the word of God spread. The number of disciples in
> Jerusalem increased rapidly, and a large number of priests
> became obedient to the faith (Acts 6:7).

With the tension between the two groups resolved, the church returned to its normal pattern of rapid growth. Luke says that the word of God spread, and that the number of believers in Jerusalem greatly increased. One estimate places the population of the city around this time at between twenty-five and thirty thousand. A significant proportion of this number must by now have belonged to the growing Christian church.

Some of these new converts were from the ranks of the

priests, vast numbers of whom were employed in the running of the temple. No doubt some of these men had lingered at the edge of the crowd which gathered daily in Solomon's Colonnade, and had been won for Christ through the anointed preaching of Peter and the other apostles. Coming to faith in Jesus as the Messiah must have had a peculiar significance for these men. They had been actively engaged in sacrificing animals, according to Old Testament law. Now they abandoned that ceaseless slaughter as they recognised in Jesus the lamb of God who, by his one atoning sacrifice, had already taken away the sin of the world.

Think about it:

1. When the apostles refused to become involved in the distribution of food, they stated that they were called to devote themselves to prayer, and to the giving out of God's Word. Do we regard these things in that order – first prayer, *then* preaching?

2. Acts 1:1 tells us that Jesus' ministry involved both teaching people and helping them in practical ways. Again we see this balance between preaching and practical help in this passage.

Some Christians are guided to minister in prayer and in the giving out of God's word. Others are called to attend to more practical affairs. Both types of activity are a ministry – a way of serving God. What is important is that we know God's will for us, and that we do it.

Pray about it:

1. Do you think of the Christian religion as something which shows you how to buy God's favour by telling you the right thing to believe, the right thing to do? If so, let these converts

from among the priests (verse 7) be an example to you. They came to see clearly that they had been accepted with God; not because of anything which they could do, but because of what Christ had already done for them on the cross.

> *Come, ye sinners, poor and wretched*
> *Weak and wounded, sick and sore:*
> *Jesus ready stands to save you*
> *Full of pity, joined with power.*
> *He is able, He is able,*
> *He is willing; doubt no more.*
>
> *Come ye weary, heavy laden*
> *Bruised and broken by the fall.*
> *If you tarry till you're better*
> *You will never come at all.*
> *Not the righteous, not the righteous;*
> *Sinners Jesus came to call.*
>
> *Lo the incarnate God ascended*
> *Pleads the merits of his blood.*
> *Venture on him, venture wholly;*
> *Let no other trust intrude.*
> *None but Jesus, none but Jesus,*
> *Can do helpless sinners good.*
>
> Joseph Hart

2. Pray that, as these priests were able to accept the gospel of Christ as the fulfilment of their Old Testament hopes, so Jews today would be brought to faith in Jesus.

The book *Betrayed* tells the story of how this happened to Stan Telchin. Stan's book was useful, in turn, to another person from a Jewish family – the famous singer from London, Helen Shapiro. When Helen was on the verge of believing in Jesus she wrote to Stan to ask if, supposing she did take this step, she would cease to be Jewish. Stan's answer was, 'It's the most Jewish thing you can do or be. Jesus didn't come to destroy the law, but to fulfil it. In the same way a Jewish person is fulfilled, or completed, in the Messiah, Jesus. When a Jewish person follows him he or she is returning to the God of Abraham, Isaac and Jacob.' Helen became a believer on the 26th of August, 1987.[12]

Almost at once, God put in her heart the burden of this prayer, 'Lord, save my people'. Pray with Helen and Stan that God would open the eyes of other Jews around the world to see in Jesus the perfect fulfilment of all their Messianic hopes.

23. Stephen Accused

Opposition arises

Now Stephen, a man full of God's grace and power, did great wonders and miraculous signs among the people. Opposition arose, however, from members of the Synagogue of the Freedmen (as it was called) – Jews of Cyrene and Alexandria as well as the provinces of Cilicia and Asia. These men began to argue with Stephen, but they could not stand up against his wisdom or the Spirit by whom he spoke (Acts 6:8-10).

The power to work miracles had won for the apostles the enthusiastic support of the people (Acts 5:12-16). The fact that Stephen now had this power must have made him popular also. But he was not popular with everyone.

'The Synagogue of the Freedmen' may refer to Jews who had been carried off as slaves from Palestine to Rome, and who had afterwards obtained their freedom. This synagogue may have been the place where these freed slaves, and after them their descendants, worshipped in Jerusalem. In any case, it was men from this synagogue who led the opposition to Stephen. In this they were joined by Jews from Cyrene (in North Africa), from Alexandria (in Egypt), from Asia (the western end of modern Turkey) and from Cilicia (the province which lay around the north east corner of the Mediterranean Sea).

The Jews from these countries would have been Greek-speaking. Stephen was involved in distributing food and clothing among the Greek-speaking Jews in Jerusalem who were Christians. It was natural that he should, in the course of his work, also come into contact with Grecian Jews from these countries who were not Christians.

These men entered into dispute with Stephen. Perhaps the debate began quietly, in a private house, though it soon became a very public affair. In this debate, the many were unable to overcome the one. Stephen received the fulfilment of the promises which Jesus had given to his disciples: 'I will give you words and wisdom that none of your adversaries will be able to resist or contradict' (Luke 21:15); 'The Holy Spirit will teach you at that time what you should say' (Luke 12:12).

By fair means or by foul

Then they secretly persuaded some men to say, 'We have heard Stephen speak words of blasphemy against Moses and against God.' So they stirred up the people and the elders and the teachers of the law. They seized Stephen and brought him before the Sanhedrin. They produced false witnesses, who testified, 'This fellow never stops speaking against the holy place and against the law. For we have heard him say that this Jesus of Nazareth will destroy this place and change the customs Moses handed down to us' (Acts 6:11-14).

Having failed to mount effective opposition to Stephen in open debate, his enemies continued their campaign by means of bribery and lies. They got hold of men who were willing to spread the rumour that they had heard Stephen blaspheming, speaking against Moses and God. Although in practice under Roman authority, Jews still regarded themselves as a people ruled by God. Blasphemy was regarded as an act of treason which carried the death sentence. It was a crime against the state, as well as an insult against Jewish religion. Once Stephen was charged with blasphemy all his good deeds were forgotten, and the people of Jerusalem combined with members of the Sanhedrin to seek him out.

We are not told what he was doing when they caught up with him. Perhaps he was encouraging believers in a private home, perhaps he was going to some house to give out clothes or food, or perhaps he was engaging in public debate. Whatever the setting, his enemies came on him with the ferocity and suddenness of an eagle swooping on its prey, and carried him off to where the Sanhedrin sat.

An unjust procedure had been set in motion and, like a juggernaut, it began to gather momentum. Instead of saying that Stephen had, perhaps on an isolated occasion, spoken against Moses and God, false witnesses now testified that he was constantly speaking against 'the holy place and the law'. The glory of God was identified in the Jewish mind with the temple, so that to say anything against the temple was to be guilty of blasphemy against God. The false witnesses, perhaps in response to prompting, now alleged that Stephen had said that Jesus would destroy the temple and would 'change the customs Moses handed down to us'.

(What Jesus actually said is recorded by Luke in chapter 21:6 of his Gospel: 'The time will come when not one stone will be left on another; every one of them will be thrown down'. So he did prophesy the destruction of the temple, though he did not say that *he* would destroy it.)

A sign from heaven

All who were sitting in the Sanhedrin looked intently at Stephen, and they saw that his face was like the face of an angel (Acts 6:15).

The charge against Stephen was serious. Luke's account communicates the rising excitement, the increasing religious fervour, the growing hatred with which Stephen was regarded. When the members of the Sanhedrin had worked themselves up to a climax of accusation and denunciation, they turned and looked as one man at the face of the accused.

They expected the mask to slip under pressure, so that they might glimpse the evil which, they were convinced, lay deep in this man's soul. On the contrary, if the mask slipped, it revealed something of the peace and holiness of heaven. He who was accused of being a traitor to Moses was singled out for sharing with Moses an honour which God had bestowed on him at Sinai (Exodus 34:29). As the loud clamour of his enemies' accusations died away, and before Stephen had spoken one word in his own defence, God gave this silent witness to his servant.

Think about it:
Luke tells us that, among those who were active in opposing Stephen were men from Cilicia. Tarsus was the capital of Cilicia. Saul was from Tarsus. Is it possible that Saul was involved in organising the opposition to Stephen right from the start, though Luke does not mention his name until Acts 7:58?

Pray about it:
This was a time of great turmoil and tension in Jerusalem. Those who regarded themselves as responsible for defending the orthodox faith felt insecure and threatened. Because they were not willing to face up to the changes which God was bringing about through the coming of Christ and the descent of the Spirit, they became entrenched and embit-

tered in their stand for the status quo. Such a situation has often developed in the history of the church. Think of John Hus in Bohemia, Latimer and Cranmer in England, George Wishart in Scotland, and many others who had to die at the hands of the old church before the Reformation came.

Pray that, whenever God intends to introduce changes today, church leaders will be given grace to accept these changes rather than oppose them.

24. Stephen Begins his Defence

What was going on?

Then the high priest asked him, 'Are these charges true?' (Acts 7:1)

This is the longest of all the speeches which Luke records in Acts. We could call it Stephen's defence. But Stephen did not aim to appease his accusers and to get himself off the hook. He was more concerned to defend the gospel of Christ than to save his own skin.

Stephen had been charged with the most heinous crimes – blaspheming against Moses and God (in that order!); dishonouring the temple and the law; and supporting a movement which would lead to the destruction of the temple and to the abandonment of those customs which Moses had been the means of setting up in Israel. From the point of view of his accusers, Stephen was touching the nerve centres both of the religion and of the national identity of the Jewish people.

Stephen's defence was, on one level, straight forward. He recounted the main points in the history of God's revelation of himself to his people. This was the simple way in which any Jew would respond to the accusation of heresy. Stephen was in effect saying, 'You rightly regard these facts of revelation history as having the greatest possible importance. I want to make it clear to you that I, too, hold these things in the highest regard. There is no difference between us on this issue.'

However there was another dimension to Stephen's speech. Time and again, while asserting the orthodox view, he did so in a way which challenged the prejudices of his accusers. All through his speech he fought for the possibility that, at the end, the members of the Sanhedrin might have their minds opened even by the tiniest crack to the thought that God had something to say to them through the gospel of Christ. His hearers saw the past as a fixed thing – facts of history and customs deriving from these facts. Stephen saw the past as the story of God's dynamic revelation of himself. He saw it as something which was alive, something which built up a momentum with the passage of time, leading irresistibly to the coming of Christ. The Christian gospel, then, was not alien to the Jewish heritage. It had grown out of it.

Abraham

To this he replied: 'Brothers and fathers, listen to me! The God of Glory appeared to our father Abraham while he was still in Mesopotamia, before he lived in Haran. "Leave your country and your people," God said, "and go to the land I will show you." So he left the land of the Chaldeans and settled in Haran. After the death of his father, God sent him to this land where you are now living. He gave him no inheritance here, not even a foot of ground. But God promised him that he and his descendants after him would possess the land, even though at that time Abraham had no child. God spoke to him in this way: "Your descendants will be strangers in a country not their own, and they will be enslaved and mistreated four hundred years. But I will punish the nation they serve as slaves," God said, "and afterwards they will come out of that country and worship me in this place." Then he gave Abraham the covenant of circumcision. And Abraham became the father of Isaac and circumcised him eight days after his birth. Later Isaac became the father of Jacob, and Jacob became the father of the twelve patriarchs' (Acts 7:2-8).

Stephen began by going straight to the father of the Jewish nation. He emphasised his unity with his accusers by referring to Abraham as 'our father'. But he also slipped in two challenging thoughts. The Jews connected 'glory' with the tabernacle, and afterwards with the temple, where the glory of God appeared (Exodus 40:34, 2 Chronicles 7:1-3). Stephen told them that the 'God of Glory' had appeared to Abraham before the tabernacle and the temple had ever been dreamed of. He also pointed out that God had revealed himself to Abraham in Mesopotamia (in that part of it which lies to the south of modern Iraq). God's revelation of himself was not confined to Canaan, as Sanhedrin members might have come to think!

Stephen went on to affirm the accepted story of Abraham's life, as recorded in the book of Genesis – how he left Ur, in the lower Euphrates valley, settled for a time in Haran, in the upper Euphrates valley, and then moved on to Canaan. His account of these events at the dawn of Jewish history was, however, distinctive in some respects. Stephen did not hero worship Abraham, nor did he glorify the promised land. He presented Abraham as a man with a living, personal, relationship with God. And Abraham did not own one inch of sacred soil!

But God did give Abraham a son, and then another precious gift – the rite of circumcision. Circumcision was not just the badge of being a Jew (the Jews were not the only people who practised this rite). Circumcision was the sign of a spiritual blessing (Romans 4:11); it was the seal of the most wonderful privilege which Abraham had – a spiritual relationship with God. This relationship came into existence within a covenant which God initiated in his grace. It was within the framework of this gracious covenant that the

Jewish nation was born. The message for Stephen's hearers was clear: 'If you are in a position of privilege before God, that position does not depend on any natural factor, but only on the supernatural grace of God.'

Joseph

'Because the patriarchs were jealous of Joseph, they sold him as a slave into Egypt. But God was with him and rescued him from all his troubles. He gave Joseph wisdom and enabled him to gain the goodwill of Pharaoh king of Egypt; so he made him ruler over Egypt and all his palace. Then a famine struck all Egypt and Canaan, bringing great suffering, and our fathers could not find food. When Jacob heard that there was grain in Egypt, he sent our fathers on their first visit. On their second visit, Joseph told his brothers who he was, and Pharaoh learned about Joseph's family. After this, Joseph sent for his father Jacob and his whole family, seventy-five in all. Then Jacob went down to Egypt, where he and our fathers died. Their bodies were brought back to Shechem and placed in the tomb that Abraham had bought from the sons of Hamor at Shechem for a certain sum of money' (Acts 7:9-16). (See Genesis chapters 37 and 39-45.)

A lot of the action in the life of Joseph took place in Egypt. When Joseph first went there, he had a rough time. Yet 'God was with him'. This is the same point as Stephen made from the story of Abraham's life. God's purposes are not tied to Canaan. To experience his grace, it is not necessary to stay within the borders of the promised land.

Stephen missed out a lot of detail from his summary of the lives of the patriarchs. Yet he chose to finish his account of this period by mentioning Shechem. Shechem was the centre of Samaritan worship. The Jews had no dealings with the Samaritans. The Sanhedrin did not even want to think about the Samaritans, but Stephen, perhaps aware that God was soon to send the gospel to Samaria, did.

Think about it:

The story of Joseph contains some striking parallels with the life of Christ. God revealed to Joseph when he was young that he was destined for greatness. Joseph's brothers were jealous of him, and sold him into slavery. But Joseph was raised to prominence in spite of what his brothers did to him. After that, he used his power and influence to preserve alive those who otherwise would have died – even the very brothers who had done him down.

When Joseph revealed himself to his estranged brothers, they were ashamed of how they had treated him. But Joseph directed their thoughts away from their sin to God's grace. 'Do not be distressed and do not be angry with yourselves for selling me here, because it was to save lives that God sent me ahead of you' (Genesis 45:5). On the basis of that statement of the grace of God, Joseph's brothers were reconciled to him. It is right for us to be ashamed of our sin. But we are called to be reconciled to God – looking, beyond our sin, to the grace of God in Christ.

We catch another glimpse of Jesus in the figure of Joseph, as we hear him say to his brothers at that time of famine, 'You shall live in the region of Goshen, and be near me .... I will provide for you there' (Genesis 45:10-11). Have we recognised in Jesus the one who alone stands between us and spiritual starvation? And are we living close to him, so that the riches of his grace are ours, not just for a moment but for ever?

25. Stephen on Moses

Moses – Part 1

'As the time drew near for God to fulfill his promise to Abraham, the number of our people in Egypt greatly increased. Then another king, who knew nothing about Joseph, became ruler of Egypt. He dealt treacherously with our people and oppressed our forefathers by forcing them to throw out their newborn babies so that they would die. At that time Moses was born, and he was no ordinary child. For three months he was cared for in his father's house. When he was placed outside, Pharaoh's daughter took him and brought him up as her own son. Moses was educated in all the wisdom of the Egyptians and was powerful in speech and action. When Moses was forty years old, he decided to visit his fellow Israelites. He saw one of them being mistreated by an Egyptian, so he went to his defense and avenged him by killing the Egyptian. Moses thought that his own people would realize that God was using him to rescue them, but they did not. The next day Moses came upon two Israelites who were fighting. He tried to reconcile them by saying, "Men, you are brothers, why do you want to hurt each other?" But the man who was mistreating the other pushed Moses aside and said, "Who made you ruler and judge over us? Do you want to kill me as you killed the Egyptian yesterday?" When Moses heard this, he fled to Midian, where he settled as a foreigner and had two sons (Acts 7:17-29). (See Exodus chapters 1 and 2, and Hebrews 11:23-27.)

Stephen's hearers worshipped the founders of their nation and their religion. Stephen wanted to show that he, too, had respect for the past. But he did it in such a way as gave glory to God, and not to any man.

In telling the story of Joseph, Stephen showed that those

within the church (Joseph's brothers) could not be trusted with the church's safety. Then he showed that those outwith the church (Pharaoh) could not be trusted to look after the church either.

In Joseph's time, Pharaoh promised that the Children of Israel would enjoy security and support in Egypt. However, with the passage of time, Pharaoh's successor turned against those to whom this promise of protection had been given. He forced the Israelites to practise population control in the crudest way.

It was into this world of danger and death that Moses was born. But his birth at such a time was no mistake. He was born then because he was most needed then. Through him, the purposes of God for the deliverance of his people were to be fulfilled.

It seems that, in some way, Moses' parents became aware of this fact. This is what led them to regard their child in a special light. It was this knowledge which enabled them to focus in faith on God rather than be bound by fear of Pharaoh. In faith they hid their child. Then, when that was no longer possible, in faith they launched him on the waters of the Nile.

And their faith was rewarded. Their child was protected. The daughter of the very man who was killing the other Hebrew children took up Moses into her arms and into her heart and into her home. Thus Moses came to receive the best education which an advanced civilisation could give. He was trained to be a leader by those very people from under whose oppressive rule he would yet lead his own people to freedom.

Years passed. Then, when Moses was forty years old, an idea was born in his heart. He went to visit his people.

It was not a pleasant experience. The world in which his people lived was one of impossible burdens, of task masters, and of cruel whips. Moses walked right into that world, and he could not cope. When he saw an Egyptian beating one of his brother Israelites, something inside him snapped. Perhaps the realisation that he was called to deliver his people suddenly came to life and lent him unnatural energy. He killed the Egyptian, and as he buried him in the sand he knew that nothing in his life could ever be the same again.

The next day, he visited his people again. This time, it was two Israelites who were fighting. Moses sought to intervene. He was so conscious of his calling to leadership that he thought it would be obvious to everyone. But it wasn't. At this first presentation of himself as the leader of his people, they rejected him. Yes, he had been called. But no, he had not been called to leadership according to his way nor at the time that he chose. The end of *Moses Part One* is like the stage in a film when the hero's first effort to deal with a problem ends in disaster. Stephen's message to the Sanhedrin was plain. There was no reason for them to worship the memory of Moses. As far as Moses himself was concerned, attempting to do something in his own strength and in his own time and way, he was a failure.

Moses – Part 2

'After forty years had passed, an angel appeared to Moses in the flames of a burning bush in the desert near Mount Sinai. When he saw this, he was amazed at the sight. As he went over to look more closely, he heard the Lord's voice: "I am the God of your fathers, the God of Abraham, Isaac and Jacob." Moses trembled with fear and did not dare to look. Then the Lord said to him, "Take off your sandals; the place where you are standing is holy ground. I have indeed seen the oppression of my people in Egypt. I have heard their groaning and have come down to set them free. Now come, I will send you back to Egypt." This is the same Moses whom they had rejected with the words, "Who made you ruler and judge?" He was sent to be their ruler and deliverer by God himself, through the angel who appeared to him in the bush. He led them out of Egypt and did wonders and miraculous signs in Egypt, at the Red Sea and for forty years in the desert. This is that Moses who told the Israelites, "God will send you a prophet like me from your own people." He was in the assembly in the desert, with the angel who spoke to him on Mount Sinai, and with our fathers; and he received living words to pass on to us' (Acts 7:30-38). (See Exodus chapter 3.)

It has been said that Moses spent 40 years thinking that he was somebody, 40 years realising that he was nobody, then 40 years finding out what God can do through a nobody. Stephen had covered the first two periods; now he came to the third.

In the silence, in the isolation of the desert, God spoke to Moses. He did this because he remembered the promises which he had made to his people, before Moses was born. He did it because he felt for them in their suffering, and could not ignore their plight. He spoke to Moses because he wanted Moses to do something about the suffering of his people.

Again Stephen, though highly selective in what material he included from the Old Testament account, emphasised one point. The fact that God spoke to Moses turned that spot into holy ground, even though it was far from the Promised Land. Not that God was calling for pilgrimages to that remote spot in the desert. What matters is not one piece of

ground as against another, but a living relationship with
God, a genuine personal openness to what he has to say,
wherever we are. Stephen's emphasis here was clearly in
contrast with his hearers' attitude of virtual temple worship.

Moses – Part 3

'But our fathers refused to obey him. Instead, they rejected
him and in their hearts turned back to Egypt. They told
Aaron, "Make us gods who will go before us. As for this
fellow Moses who led us out of Egypt – we don't know what
has happened to him!" That was the time they made an idol
in the form of a calf. They brought sacrifices to it and held
a celebration in honour of what their hands had made. But
God turned away and gave them over to the worship of the
heavenly bodies. This agrees with what is written in the
book of the prophets: "Did you bring me sacrifices and
offerings for forty years in the desert, O house of Israel? You
have lifted up the shrine of Molech and the star of your god
Rephan, the idols you made to worship. Therefore I will send
you into exile beyond Babylon"' (Acts 7:39-43).

Stephen's hearers boasted in the memory of their forebears.
But, reviewing how these forebears had actually behaved in
the wilderness, Stephen showed that there was no basis for
this boasting.

Their forebears did not listen to Moses. Having rejected
God's word through his servant, they slid back towards that
depraved condition in which they had lived before coming
out of Egypt. Instead of accepting the fact that the God who
revealed himself from Sinai was a *spirit*, they craved after
something physical. Instead of accepting the revelation
which God had given, they clamoured for something which
they could call their own.

Because they turned away from God, God turned away from them. Because they chose to reject his law and his grace, God gave them up to their own sin. A spiritual gulf opened up between God and those who professed to follow him. Through time this spiritual estrangement was expressed outwardly, when God's people were uprooted from the Promised Land and were driven away to exile in Babylon.

Think about it:
Seeking to point his hearers to Jesus, Stephen quoted Deuteronomy 18:15, where Moses foretold the coming of another prophet who would be like him. Think about the parallels between Moses and Jesus.

Moses was born at a time when there was death in the air. So Herod the Great, jealous of the child king, tried to kill Jesus at birth. Moses was called from among the people of Israel: so was Jesus. Moses had an intimate relationship with God: so had Jesus. Moses was the means of bringing God's word to God's people: so was Jesus. The word which God communicated through Moses was alive and life-giving: so is the word which God gives to us through Jesus.

All this adds up to the fact that Moses was a mediator between God and men: so is Jesus. In fact one of Moses' main functions was to point forward to him whom Paul describes as the 'one mediator between God and men, the man Christ Jesus' (I Timothy 2:5).

Pray about it:
Moses was miraculously preserved at birth, then uniquely prepared to lead God's people. Yet, when the time came for God to call him into leadership, he was unwilling to respond.

If God calls you to serve him, are you willing to obey?

26. The First Christian Martyr

The tabernacle and the temple

'Our forefathers had the tabernacle of the Testimony with
them in the desert. It had been made as God directed Moses,
according to the pattern he had seen. Having received the
tabernacle, our fathers under Joshua brought it with them when
they took the land from the nations God drove out before them.
It remained in the land until the time of David, who enjoyed
God's favour and asked that he might provide a dwelling place
for the God of Jacob. But it was Solomon who built the house
for him. However, the Most High does not live in houses made
by men. As the prophet says: "Heaven is my throne, and the
earth is my footstool. What kind of house will you build for
me? says the Lord. Or where will my resting place be? Has not
my hand made all these things?" ' (Acts 7:44-50).

Speaking of the era when the tabernacle was the centre of
Israel's worship, Stephen made two points.

Firstly the simple tabernacle, which was erected and
taken down many times in the course of Israel's journey
through the wilderness, was clearly according to the will of
God. So, although the members of the Sanhedrin thought
that the huge, impressive buildings of the temple were indis-
pensable, God did not.

Secondly, as long as Israel showed their obedience to
God by worshipping him according to his will, they enjoyed
his presence and blessing. God gave them victory over their
enemies, and ensured for them a safe entry into the Promised
Land.

In speaking of the temple Stephen was approaching a
particularly sensitive subject, one which featured in the

charges made against him (Acts 6:13-14). According to these charges, Stephen had foretold massive changes in the worship of God, including the destruction of the temple. In referring to the change from tabernacle to temple, Stephen may have been making the relevant point – 'There was change in the way in which God was worshipped even in Old Testament times. Why do you react in such panic at the very suggestion of change? Now that the Messiah has come, should we not expect some changes?'

As to the building of the temple Stephen said that, although David wanted to carry out this project, God postponed it till the days of Solomon. Stephen's point may again have been that, although his accusers regarded the temple as of absolute and abiding religious importance, God himself had shown that it was something he could do without.

One point which Stephen made in the clearest way was that God was greater than the temple. Even in the days of Solomon and of the prophet Isaiah (from whom Stephen quoted), God had made this abundantly clear. To the Sanhedrin members whose religion consisted in external ritual, the temple was first and God second. But Stephen asserted, as Scripture had always taught, that God alone came first.

The accusers accused

'You stiff-necked people, with uncircumcised hearts and ears! You are just like your fathers: You always resist the Holy Spirit! Was there ever a prophet your fathers did not persecute? They even killed those who predicted the coming of the Righteous One. And now you have betrayed and murdered him – you who have received the law that was put into effect through angels but have not obeyed it' (Acts 7:51-53).

They were many, and he was alone. They exercised the authority of the highest court in Israel, in church and state, while he was without any official influence. But, as Stephen's speech came to its climax under the guidance of the Spirit, the tables were turned. Those who had accused him of capital offences were themselves accused of the most heinous sin.

Their fathers had been given the Law, but they had rejected it. God had then sent his prophets, but they had rejected them. Lastly God had sent his Son. But the Sanhedrin, representing the whole nation, had rejected him also. Thus Stephen accused his accusers of resisting the Spirit, as their fathers had done before them.

'Receive my spirit'

When they heard this, they were furious and gnashed their teeth at him. But Stephen, full of the Holy Spirit, looked up to heaven and saw the glory of God, and Jesus standing at the right hand of God. 'Look,' he said, 'I see heaven open and the Son of Man standing at the right hand of God.' At this they covered their ears and, yelling at the top of their voices, they all rushed at him, dragged him out of the city and began to stone him. Meanwhile, the witnesses laid their clothes at the feet of a young man named Saul. While they were stoning him, Stephen prayed, 'Lord Jesus, receive my spirit.' Then he fell on his knees and cried out, 'Lord, do not hold this sin against them.' When he had said this, he fell asleep (Acts 7:54-60).

As Stephen spoke, the members of the Sanhedrin gnashed their teeth like wild animals in pain.

They were grieving the Spirit, even as he himself was being filled with the Spirit. The fact that he was full of the

Spirit was mentioned when we were told about his being chosen as one of the seven (Acts 6:5). It is mentioned again here. Being filled with the Spirit is not like being filled with air, as a balloon is. It is like being filled as a pipe which conducts water to a home. The pipe needs to be filled again and again.

The work of the Spirit is to focus our attention on Jesus. Arriving at a church to speak on the words, 'He shall glorify me', J. I. Packer found his message already illustrated by the flood lights which highlighted the church building on that dark winter's night.[13] You do not visit a site to look at the flood lights. Their function is to direct attention away from themselves. It comes as no surprise then to know that Stephen, filled with the Spirit, was thinking of Jesus, and talking of Jesus. He was even seeing Jesus.

He describes Jesus as 'the son of man'. Jesus had used this description of himself when he had stood before this same court: 'In the future you will see the Son of Man sitting at the right hand of the Mighty One' (Matthew 26:64). Jesus is usually represented in Scripture as sitting at God's right hand, but Stephen perceived him to be standing. This might mean that, while the supreme court of the Jewish church and nation condemned Stephen on earth, Jesus himself rose to speak on his behalf in heaven. It could also mean that Jesus was rising to receive him into heaven. This sight must have afforded indescribable comfort to Stephen as he was led off down a lonely road to a painful death.

Stephen's triumphant cry was, in effect, an appeal to a higher court. But the members of the Sanhedrin would have none of it. Putting their hands over their ears and raising their voices, they sought to protect themselves from defilement through hearing a prayer addressed to the one whom they rejected. Then they hurried this man out of their city and purged themselves of his company as their society had purged itself of blasphemers from ancient times (Deuteronomy 17:7). In accordance with the law, the witnesses against Stephen were the first to cast stones at him. It was hot work. The witnesses took off their outer clothes. They laid them, for safe keeping, at the feet of Saul.

Saul, from Tarsus in Cilicia, may have come up against Stephen along with others from that part who disputed with him (Acts 6:9). He certainly agreed with what was being done here, outside Jerusalem. He may even have acted as herald, proclaiming the nature of Stephen's offence and the fact that he was now to die for it. Luke wants us to note well this face in that crowd.

Meanwhile Stephen was calling on the name of the Saviour whom he had just seen at God's right hand in heaven. As Jesus had asked his Father to receive his spirit in the moment of death (Luke 23:46), Stephen now asked Jesus to do that for him. Also, as Jesus had prayed for the forgiveness of his enemies (Luke 23:34), Stephen likewise prayed for those who were putting him to death.

And so, surrounded by an atmosphere of unrest and of hatred, he fell asleep in a spirit of peace and of love. A little bit of heaven, surrounded by a lot of hell.

Think about it:

1. In 1415, John Hus of Bohemia was condemned for preaching the gospel in opposition to the authority of the church. As he prepared to be burned at the stake outside the city of Constance, he repeatedly quoted the words of Psalm 31:5: 'Into your hands I commit my spirit; redeem me, O LORD, the God of truth.' He also prayed that those who had

accused him falsely would be forgiven. Jesus, Stephen and John Hus were travelling light towards death. They had committed their spirits to God, and they carried no burden of resentment towards their enemies. Are we travelling as lightly as they were?

2. Stephen might have felt that he was being dragged off to death with half his life's work undone. Yet he was able to go willingly, as running into the arms of Jesus.

James Templeton, an Aberdeen minister who died in 1840, was once speaking to his congregation about how he had noted an unwillingness to die among some believers. 'It just reminds me,' he said, 'of what happened when I left the auld hoose. When a' the furniture was oot, and a' the rest had gane to the new ane, I couldna leave. I paced up and doon the room in which my children were born; I gazed on the wa's of the chamber where I studied and wrestled with God, and I couldna tear myself away. But Betty the servant came and she said, *Come awa', sir, come awa'. The time's up, and the ither hoose is far better than this.*'[14]

Pray about it:
For the members of the Sanhedrin, the temple was the central element in a religion which was dominated by external things. One safeguard against such a religion is, to remember that the church itself is the temple of God.

Pray that, as part of God's living temple, you will daily be cleansed from sin and filled with his Spirit.

27. Persecution with a Purpose

A study in contrasts

> And Saul was there, giving approval to his death ... Godly
> men buried Stephen and mourned deeply for him. But Saul
> began to destroy the church. Going from house to house,
> he dragged off men and women and put them in prison
> (Acts 8:1a, 2-3).

Luke wants us to feel the sharp contrast between Stephen,
whose death he has just described, and Saul, who was
involved in his murder.

Stephen was filled with the Spirit (Acts 6:5, 7:55); Saul
was grieving the Spirit (Acts 7:51). As a murderer, and as a
man filled with malice towards others, Saul was burdened
with guilt. Stephen was free from resentment towards any
man, even towards those who killed him. Stephen lived and
died for Christ; Saul persecuted Christ, in the person of
those who believed in him (Acts 9:4).

Although Stephen was surrounded by men of violence,
and died a violent death, Luke's description conveys the
atmosphere of gentleness and peace in which Stephen ended
his life. Then we hear the slow step of those who laid his
body to rest, weeping hot tears of love. But Saul went raging
round Jerusalem like a wild bull – trampling, goring, tossing
believers all over the place.

He rides upon the storm

> On that day a great persecution broke out against the
> church at Jerusalem, and all except the apostles were
> scattered throughout Judea and Samaria .... Those who had

been scattered preached the word wherever they went
(Acts 8:1b,4).

Luke's consuming interest is the expansion of the early
church. He has described the church's establishment in
Jerusalem, and its initial growth. But he wants to get out of
Jerusalem, he wants to tell us the story of how the gospel of
Christ moved out to conquer the world.

From the human point of view, these believers were
thrown out of Jerusalem like some unfortunate matador in
a Spanish ring, caught on the end of a bull's horn and tossed
up into the crowd. From the divine point of view, these
believers were scattered like seed which God picked up in
his hand and threw out with a view to a harvest yet to come.

The fact that the word of God *would* go out from
Jerusalem to the world had been foretold, for example in
Micah 4:2, 'The law will go out from Zion, the word of the
Lord from Jerusalem.' The fact that God's word *should* go
out from the church to the world had been taught by Jesus,
for example in Matthew 28:19, 'Go and make disciples of all
nations'. But the fact also remains that the gospel would not
have gone out so quickly if believers had not been forced out
of Jerusalem by persecution.

The Rev. Dr. John Philip was minister of a church in
Aberdeen from 1804-1818. Towards the end of that successful ministry he had a debate with an atheist. When this
man attacked Dr. Philip's faith, the minister defended
himself effectively. However, having lost the argument, the
atheist did in a sense have the last word. 'You profess to
believe that untold millions are perishing in ignorance,' he
said. 'And yet you are living in comparative ease and
comfort, addressing a few of your fellow creatures.'[15] This

taunt, combined with other factors, was the means of Dr. Philip's leaving Aberdeen to become a missionary in South Africa. God uses even his enemies to accomplish his purposes.

> *God moves in a mysterious way*
> *His wonders to perform;*
> *He plants His footsteps in the sea,*
> *And rides upon the storm.*
>   William Cowper

Think about it:
In the Old Testament, most movement seems to have been inward. Pilgrims gathered for the annual feasts to Jerusalem, the centre of Jewish life. If there was any outreach, it seems to have involved bringing outsiders in to a place of blessing. In the New Testament, by contrast, the direction of movement is outward. The church moves out from Jerusalem, bringing the gospel to the world outside. It is not now so much a matter of bringing people in to a place of blessing, wherever that is, as of bringing blessing to people, wherever they are. What attitude do we have to missionary work – do we think of bringing people *in*, as they did in the Old Testament; or do we think of carrying the gospel *out*, as the early church learned to do?

Kierkegaard invites us to think about the same question, though he expresses it in a different way: 'It is in the living room that the battle must be fought, lest the religious conflict degenerate into a parade of the guard once a week; in the living room must the battle be fought, not fantastically in the church, so that the clergyman is fighting windmills and the spectators watch the show; in the living room the battle must be fought, for the victory consists precisely in the living room becoming a sanctuary.'[16]

Pray about it:
If you are suffering for your faith in Christ, how are you reacting? During Idi Amin's reign of terror in Uganda in the 1970s, Bishop Festo Kivengere was asked how he would react if he were handed a gun and Amin were sitting opposite him. Festo said, 'The only reply that I could give is that I would hand the gun to the President and say, 'I think this is your weapon. It is not mine. My weapon is love.'" On other occasions Festo said about Amin, 'A bullet can kill, but a bullet cannot heal ... I am just learning to forgive. If I don't love, I am the loser.'[17]

28. The Gospel goes North

Philip went down to a city in Samaria and proclaimed the
Christ there. When the crowds heard Philip and saw the
miraculous signs he did, they all paid close attention to
what he said. With shrieks, evil spirits came out of many,
and many paralytics and cripples were healed. So there
was great joy in that city (Acts 8:5-8).

Philip was one of the seven chosen along with Stephen (Acts
6:5). In Acts 21:8, he is described as an evangelist.

The country of Samaria lay to the north of Judea. It is
uncertain to which Samaritan town it was that Philip went.
It may have been Shechem. If so, Philip was preaching the
gospel at the very centre of the Samaritan religion.

Many barriers
The history of Samaria went back to the time when the
kingdom of the twelve tribes of Israel split up, after the death
of Solomon (2 Chronicles chapter 10). The vast majority
adhered to the northern kingdom, which came to be called
Israel. The minority adhered to the southern kingdom,
which came to be called Judah.

After about two centuries of its separate existence, the
northern kingdom of Israel was invaded by the Assyrians.
Many Israelites were deported to various parts of the Assyr-
ian empire, and many people from other parts of the empire
were imported to Israel. This meant that the religion of the
northern kingdom became a mixture of Judaism and pagan-
ism (2 Kings 17:24, 34).

Later, when the people of Judah returned from exile in
Babylon and began to rebuild the temple in Jerusalem,

members of the northern kingdom (now called Samaritans) offered to help them. However, because the religion of the Samaritans had become so impure, this offer was refused (Ezra 4:1-3). The Samaritans, greatly offended, then built their own temple on Mount Gerizim.

By the time that Philip was called to preach the gospel in Samaria, there were many barriers between him and these people in the north. The current attitude was, 'Jews do not associate with Samaritans' (John 4:9).

One bridge *(see John 4:1-42)*

The bridge across the barriers of history, of culture and of religion was Christ. Especially if Philip was preaching at Shechem, the centre of Samaritan religion with the temple nearby on Mount Gerizim, he could have criticised the Samaritans for their impure religion. But instead of that he preached Christ to them.

Not far from Shechem was the town of Sychar, where Jesus met the Samaritan woman. This woman came to recognise in Jesus the fulfilment of the Samaritans' expectation that a Messiah would come. (Although their religion was impure, the Samaritans did adhere to the Pentateuch, with its prophecy of a Messiah in Deuteronomy 18:15. Many other Samaritans in that area also came to believe in Jesus. Perhaps these people spoke to others, so that by the time Philip arrived there were many who were ready and eager to hear his message.)

Philip's ministry in Samaria was supported by signs of the healing power of God, just as the ministry of Jesus had been (Matthew 4:24), and as the ministry of the apostles was in Jerusalem (Acts 5:16). As a result, the people of Samaria listened all the more attentively to what Philip preached.

And as they listened, they experienced a joy which they had
never known before.

A sorcerer joins the church

Now for some time a man named Simon had practiced
sorcery in the city and amazed all the people of Samaria.
He boasted that he was someone great, and all the people,
both high and low, gave him their attention and exclaimed,
'This man is the divine power known as the Great Power.'
They followed him because he had amazed them for a long
time with his magic. But when they believed Philip as he
preached the good news of the kingdom of God and the
name of Jesus Christ, they were baptised, both men and
women. Simon himself believed and was baptised. And he
followed Philip everywhere, astonished by the great signs
and miracles he saw (Acts 8:9-13).

The Samaritans heard the good news about Jesus, the long
promised Messiah, and they believed in him. As they
believed in him, they were baptised. That is, they acknowledged that they did not belong to themselves any more. They
belonged to Jesus now. Thus the church in Samaria grew.
Among those who joined was a man who had cast a long
shadow over that whole area – Simon the sorcerer.

Simon said that he was someone great. The people of
Samaria went further, saying that the power of the Supreme
Being rested on and worked through him.

Simon may have had some scientific knowledge. He may
have used his superior knowledge of nature to support his
claim to possess unusual powers. Alongside such knowledge, Satan was no doubt working through Simon, to keep
the people of Samaria in bondage. When Samaria was soon
to hear about the kingdom of God, and about the Messiah

through whom the saving power of God was to be felt, perhaps Satan set Simon up, complete with signs and wonders – a false Messiah to confuse the Samaritans, to prejudice them against the true Messiah whom Philip was about to preach.

Then Philip arrived from Jerusalem, and the real power of God came to town. This preacher was not just someone with superior knowledge of nature. He was certainly not in league with Satan. He was from God, he was preaching the good news of the kingdom of God, and the power of God was felt through his ministry. Simon the sorcerer was enthralled. It was not so much the preaching of the gospel which impressed him; it was more the miracles which accompanied Philip's preaching. Philip seemed to be in league with a power far superior to anything that Simon had previously experienced. He gave up what he had been doing, and followed Philip around. Along with many other Samaritans, he professed faith in Christ and was baptised.

A deputation from Jerusalem

> When the apostles in Jerusalem heard that Samaria had accepted the word of God, they sent Peter and John to them. When they arrived, they prayed for them that they might receive the Holy Spirit, because the Holy Spirit had not yet come upon any of them; they had simply been baptised into the name of the Lord Jesus. Then Peter and John placed their hands on them, and they received the Holy Spirit (Acts 8:14-17).

This is John's last appearance in the book of Acts. It is not surprising that he made it in Peter's company. Their friendship went back a long way.

Now they came up together from Jerusalem, to see what God was doing in Samaria. It must have been difficult for them, as it had no doubt been for Philip, to cross these barriers. Christ alone made such a trip possible.

When they got to Samaria, they laid hands on those who had joined the church and prayed for them. It was a gesture by which the Jewish apostles accepted the Samaritan believers as part of the same church; and it expressed the apostles' desire that these Samaritan believers would receive more blessing yet. Jewish hands, resting in acceptance and in blessing on Samaritan heads – with God, all things are possible!

These Samaritans had already received the Holy Spirit. Paul says that, although a gift like the gift of tongues was not given to everyone in the Corinthian church, every believer in the Corinthian church was nevertheless a partaker of the Holy Spirit (1 Corinthians 12:11-13). However, on the Day of Pentecost, those who were already believers in the Jerusalem church received the Spirit in a new way. He came with signs to demonstrate the fact that this was the age of the Spirit, and to bring home the fact that the evangelising of the nations of the world could, and would, be done. His presence in the church, his powerful working through the church, would bring it to pass.

It was particularly appropriate that the signs which accompanied the descent of the Spirit at Pentecost in Jerusalem should, at least to some extent, be repeated in Samaria. Centuries of division called for the fullest demonstration of the fact that, in Christ, Jerusalem and Samaria were now one. (On the same basis, the closing of the gap between Jew and Gentile was to be sealed and celebrated in the granting of Pentecostal gifts to the Gentiles whose coming to faith in

Christ is recounted in Acts chapter 10. Acts 8 and Acts 10 are thus in a sense the completion of Acts 2. They tell us about the extension of Pentecost to Samaria and to the whole Gentile world.)

Simon exposed

> When Simon saw that the Spirit was given at the laying on of the apostles' hands, he offered them money and said, 'Give me also this ability so that everyone on whom I lay my hands may receive the Holy Spirit.' Peter answered: 'May your money perish with you, because you thought you could buy the gift of God with money! You have no part or share in this ministry, because your heart is not right before God. Repent of this wickedness and pray to the Lord. Perhaps he will forgive you for having such a thought in your heart. For I see that you are full of bitterness and captive to sin.' Then Simon answered, 'Pray to the Lord for me so that nothing you have said may happen to me' (Acts 8:18-24).

Verse 13 suggests that Simon was more impressed by the miracles which he saw than by the gospel which he heard. Verse 18 mentions again the impact which the signs of the Spirit had on Simon. It was not that the gospel was taking hold of him, but that he wanted to take hold of the miraculous power which accompanied the preaching of the gospel. Perhaps Simon had given good money to a master magician, who had initiated him into the art of illusion. Probably he had been paid by clients who had come to him in the hope that he could help them. Looking at the dramatic gifts of the Spirit which he saw to accompany the apostles' ministry, Simon could foresee a wonderful future. If he needed to pay, he was willing to pay. He was sure that the consequent increase in his influence as a sorcerer would fully justify this investment. If Peter would only teach him how to do this trick ....

Peter's response was sudden and sharp. He denounced Simon's suggestion as being completely out of harmony with the will of God. He exposed Simon himself as someone who just did not belong in this kingdom of grace which God was extending to Samaria. However he did not leave the door of hope completely closed. He called on Simon to repent. The last glimpse we get of Simon, he is asking Peter to pray for him.

A fitting exit

> When they had testified and proclaimed the word of the Lord, Peter and John returned to Jerusalem, preaching the gospel in many Samaritan villages (Acts 8:25).

Jesus was once refused entry to a Samaritan village. James and John, incensed at the offence offered to their Master, spoke of bringing fire down from heaven on these Samaritans (Luke 9:51-55). Now John showed a different spirit. He and Peter reached out and touched Samaritans, they prayed for them, they went round the country preaching to them the gospel of peace. A fitting exit from the Book of Acts for John, who was to become known as 'the apostle of love'.

Think about it:
1. Luke says in verse 13 that Simon believed. From what Peter subsequently says, however, it seems that Simon was not a genuine believer. How can we resolve this conflict?

In the parable of the sower, Jesus speaks of some who hear the gospel but who are like ground in which there is, under the surface, a layer of solid rock. Of such hearers Jesus

says, 'They believe for a while, but in time of testing they
fall away' (Luke 8:13). The word of God is there on the
surface, and these people do in a sense believe it. But it has
not really penetrated their hearts, which are still hardened in
sin. Simon seems to have been such a believer.

2. Though Peter spoke in such a forceful way to Simon he
was careful to point him to the mercy of God, and not to
leave him wallowing in despair.

An artist once painted a picture in which two figures were
seated beside a table, playing a game of chess. Actually, the
game was over; the title of the painting was *Checkmate*. One
figure represented the devil. The other was a young man.
The message portrayed by the painting was that the devil
had outwitted the young man, and that he now had no way
of escape.

One day a visitor entered the gallery where this painting
was hanging. As a master chess player, he was attracted to
this painting. He studied the pieces as they were portrayed
on the board, then took a miniature chess set out of his
pocket and arranged the pieces as they were set out in the
painting. After a while he shouted, 'But the game is not
finished – there is still a way out!'

Whenever we become aware of our sin, Satan tries to
drive us towards despair. He wants us to believe that there
is no way out. But, through the mercy of God in Christ, there
is – even if our sins are as great as those of Simon the
sorcerer.

Pray about it:
Offering to pay for blessings accompanying the gospel,
Simon showed that he was completely out of tune with the

basic message of the gospel. Have we grasped that every aspect of salvation comes to us by the free grace of God, or not at all?

An American missionary went to India and made friends with a pearl diver called Rambouh. He tried to explain the gospel to this man, but the response was always along the lines: 'I feel that I need to pay for my place in heaven.'

When Rambouh was old, he decided to go on a pilgrimage to a Hindu holy place. He was to make this journey on his knees. The pain he would suffer would help to pay for his salvation. Before he left, he told the missionary that he wanted to give him the present of a very precious pearl. The missionary offered to pay for it, but Rambouh refused. The missionary tried to insist, but Rambouh became angry.

'You do not understand,' he said. 'This pearl belonged to my son. He was the best pearl diver on the coast. But, in obtaining this pearl, he stayed too long down on the sea bed. After he came up, he died. This pearl cost my son his life. The value of the pearl is the value of the life of my son. You cannot pay for it. Either you receive it as a gift or you do not receive it at all.'

The missionary was silent, as he understood. Then he turned to Rambouh again and said, 'That is just like the gospel of God's grace. God offers us salvation and eternal life, because Jesus died to bear away our sin. The value of salvation is the value of the life of God's son. We cannot pay for it. Either we accept it as a gift or we cannot have it at all.'

Now it was Rambouh's turn to be silent. At last he said, 'I see it now.'

Have you seen it yet?

29. The Gospel goes South

Surprising guidance

Now an angel of the Lord said to Philip, 'Go south to the road
– the desert road – that goes down from Jerusalem to Gaza.' So
he started out, and on his way he met an Ethiopian eunuch, an
important official in charge of all the treasury of Candace,
queen of the Ethiopians. This man had gone to Jerusalem to
worship, and on his way home was sitting in his chariot reading
the book of Isaiah the prophet. The Spirit told Philip, 'Go to
that chariot and stay near it.' Then Philip ran up to the chariot
and heard the man reading Isaiah the prophet. 'Do you understand what you are reading?' Philip asked. 'How can I,' he
said, 'unless someone explains it to me?' So he invited Philip
to come up and sit with him (Acts 8:26-31).

Jesus tells us that the angels are interested in the conversion
of sinners to God (Luke 15:10). Luke tells us, here and
elsewhere, that angels were actively involved in supporting
and guiding the church as it carried out God's call to preach
the gospel of Christ to the world. In Philip's case, the angel's
guidance was very specific. It seems that there were at least
two roads which one could take from Jerusalem to Gaza.
The angel told Philip which one to take. He seems to have
guided him to take the old road, which by now was hardly
used.

Philip was no doubt surprised to be told by the angel to
leave Samaria. Were things not happening in Samaria?
Were many people not coming to faith in Christ? Why
should he withdraw from this centre of gospel activity to
some deserted spot?

But he obeyed, and he was rewarded. Here, on this old

133

road, was the chariot of an official in high office from Ethiopia. Philip had been involved in evangelising the Samaritans, but now he was to evangelise someone from even further away.

How this man had become interested in the Jewish religion we are not told. Luke tells us that he was returning from Jerusalem, where he had been to worship. Perhaps he had made this long journey to be present at one of the feasts in the Jewish calendar. (If he was literally a eunuch, he would not have been allowed to approach the temple nearer than the gate to the Court of the Gentiles.) The fact that he was now reading a scroll of the book of Isaiah suggests that this man was still searching. He had made that long journey, but he still had not found what he was looking for. Perhaps he had chosen the old, deserted road to Gaza so that his driver could slow the chariot to walking pace and the eunuch could get peace and comfort to read.

The fact that the chariot was moving slowly gave Philip the chance to catch up with it. As he came near, he heard the voice of someone reading. The voice was hesitant, not moving through the passage with confidence. (The scroll would have been difficult to read, apart from any problem with the meaning, because the words would have been written without a space between them, and without punctuation.) Philip seems to have listened for a time, the eunuch too absorbed to notice him, before asking, 'You don't understand what you are reading, do you?'

The eunuch must have been astonished that someone had crept up on him in this quiet spot. He could have been offended that a person of lower rank had broken social custom by beginning a conversation with him. But he had only one thing on his mind, and was glad that anyone would join him in talking about it. He invited Philip up into the chariot.

Perfectly planned

> The eunuch was reading this passage of Scripture: 'He was led like a sheep to the slaughter, and as a lamb before the shearer is silent, so he did not open his mouth. In his humiliation he was deprived of justice. Who can speak of his descendants? For his life was taken from the earth.' The eunuch asked Philip, 'Tell me, please, who is the prophet talking about, himself or someone else?' Then Philip began with that very passage of Scripture and told him the good news about Jesus (Acts 8:32-35).

The moment when Philip met the Ethiopian was perfectly planned. He could not have been reading a more appropriate passage of Scripture than that one, speaking as it did about the sufferings and death of the Servant of the Lord. Philip did not need to roll the scroll one inch forward or back. He proclaimed Jesus to the eunuch from that very passage. That does not mean that he limited himself to that Scripture. After his resurrection, Jesus had directed the disciples to passages in all the sections of the Old Testament which pointed forward to him (Luke 24:27, 45). Philip probably did something of the same. But such a tour of the Old Testament could not have had a better starting point than Isaiah 53.

The same passage which came to mean so much to the Ethiopian is still being used today, to bring people to faith in Christ. Richard Ganz is a Jew who was born in New York City. He grew up very committed to Judaism, but when his father died his personal faith was shattered. He trained as a clinical psychologist and became very cynical and hard. He still had this cynical outlook when, in his 25th year, he went on a trip to Europe. Yet many events combined to lead him to a Christian centre in the Netherlands. There, someone read Isaiah chapter 53 to Richard. He admitted that the words could refer to the death of Christ, but he dismissed this by saying, 'Anyone at the cross could have written that. What does that prove?' The man who had read the passage said nothing, but passed Richard the Bible from which he had just read. Richard took in the fact that the passage had been written hundreds of years before the death of Christ. 'In that instant of confrontation, I knew that God demanded everything.'[19]

There and then

> As they travelled along the road, they came to some water and the eunuch said, 'Look, here is water. Why shouldn't I be baptised?' And he gave orders to stop the chariot. Then both Philip and the eunuch went down into the water and Philip baptised him (Acts 8:36-37).

Philip began to speak to the eunuch on the basis of Isaiah chapter 53. He must have said a lot more to him than what is contained in that passage. He must have said something about baptism. As soon as water came into view the eunuch said, 'Look, here is water' – as if that was precisely what they had been talking about.

The open confession of Jesus as his Saviour and Lord might have the most far-reaching consequences for the Ethiopian, personally and professionally, but he was eager to take this important step. Receiving the first Gentile into the church by the sacrament of baptism could also have repercussions for Philip. But he did not hesitate either. He

had not been rendered bitter and cynical by his disappoint-
ment with Simon the sorcerer. He had not lost his nerve. He
did not say to the eunuch, 'There are apostles up in Jerusalem. Would you mind wheeling the chariot around? Can you
spare a couple of days? We can go up to Jerusalem, and the
decision to accept you into the church will then rest with
men who have more authority than I have.' He went down
with the eunuch and baptised him there and then.

With joy in his heart

> When they came up out the water, the Spirit of the Lord
> suddenly took Philip away, and the eunuch did not see him
> again, but went on his way rejoicing. Philip, however, ap-
> peared at Azotus and travelled about, preaching the gospel in
> all the towns until he reached Caesarea (Acts 8:39-40).

God had brought them together for a glorious purpose.
(Thinking of the Ethiopian's influential position in his
home country, who could tell how significant that purpose
might yet turn out to be?) But, now that his immediate
purpose had been fulfilled, the same God as had brought
them together now drove them apart.

Philip was next seen at Azotus (the Ashdod of the Old
Testament). This was the next town, travelling north from
Gaza. Having visited other towns on the Plain of Sharon, he
seems to have settled on the coast of Caesarea (Acts 21:8).

The Ethiopian went on his way, travelling to his country,
back to his culture and to his people. And he went with joy
in his heart. The gospel had not introduced a dislocation into
his life, as if he could not be an Ethiopian *and* a Christian.
It had not crippled him, making him dependent on the man
who had preached the gospel to him. Philip had gone his

way, but the Ethiopian could go his way with dignity and self-composure. His Saviour and Lord, into whose name he had been baptised, into whose possession he had now passed, was going with him.

Think about it:

The question of the admission of Gentiles, and the terms on which they would be received into the church, was to become a big issue. Yet Philip fully and formally received this Ethiopian before anyone had even considered that there might be a problem here! Does this suggest that many of the issues which take up time and talk in the church are problems of the church's own making?

Another issue which was to divide the church in later years is, the mode of baptism. Yet this passage, again, simply does not make an issue of it!

Pray about it:

1. Philip was preaching in Samaria, to the north of Jerusalem. This man from Ethiopia was on a road to the south of Jerusalem. The apostles were nearer to him than Philip was. Yet God wanted Philip to make this contact. Philip may have felt reluctant to go, either because he wanted to carry on the work which was going so well in Samaria, or because he felt that one of the apostles, who were nearer to the area in question, would deal with this matter in a more effective way.

But, whatever he may have thought, Philip obeyed God's call. Pray that, whatever God asks you to do, you will get grace to be obedient as Philip was.

2. Captain John Coutts was the rough, tough, master of a sailing ship. When his ship was far from his home in England, he became fatally ill. He sent for any member of the crew who had a Bible, to read some verses to him. The only member of the crew who had a Bible was a boy called Willie Platt. Willie had been taught by his mother to read Isaiah 53, so he read these verses to his dying captain. Gaining some confidence, Willie said, 'My mother taught me to put my own name in here, sir. Will I read it again, putting in my name?' The captain agreed, and Willie read the passage again. 'Surely he took up Willie Platt's infirmities and carried Willie Platt's sorrows ....' Captain Coutts could see the relevance of this passage to him. The cabin boy grew even bolder and asked, 'Will I read it again, sir, and put your name in?'

'Do that, boy,' the captain said. So Willie read the passage again, '... he was pierced for Captain Coutts transgressions, he was crushed for Captain Coutts iniquities; the punishment that brought Captain Coutts peace was upon him, and by his wounds Captain Coutts is healed.'

On that lonely stretch of ocean, Captain Coutts took to himself the same words as the Ethiopian had appropriated on that deserted road south of Jerusalem. Have you come to see your need of such a drastic remedy as this – Jesus dying for you – and have you found peace with God through faith in him?

30. On the Road to Damascus

Baying for the blood of believers

> Meanwhile, Saul was still breathing out murderous threats against the Lord's disciples. He went to the high priest and asked him for letters to the synagogues in Damascus, so that if he found any there who belonged to the Way, whether men or women, he might take them as prisoners to Jerusalem (Acts 9:1-2).

Our last glimpse of Saul was in 8:3, where Luke painted a picture of him savaging the church like a wild animal. Here, Luke describes him as living in an atmosphere of threats and murder, or as giving off the odour of such things. Saul may have acted as an official agent of the Sanhedrin at the execution of Stephen (7:58). He certainly became the chief executive in Jerusalem of the policy of persecution which was adopted from the day of Stephen's death. But now he went to the High Priest, as president of the Sanhedrin, for papers authorising him to pursue believers to Damascus. This was possible because the Romans had granted to the Sanhedrin extradition rights over Jews who lived abroad and whom the Sanhedrin wished to bring back for trial to Jerusalem. Saul's appetite for the blood of believers was not easily satisfied.

A voice from the world of love

> As he neared Damascus on his journey, suddenly a light from heaven flashed around him. He fell to the ground and heard a voice say to him, 'Saul, Saul, why do you persecute me?' 'Who are you, Lord?' Saul asked. 'I am Jesus, whom you are

persecuting,' he replied. 'Now get up and go into the city, and you will be told what you must do.' The men travelling with Saul stood there speechless; they heard the sound but did not see anyone. Saul got up from the ground, but when he opened his eyes he could see nothing. So they led him by the hand into Damascus. For three days he was blind, and did not eat or drink anything (Acts 9:3-9).

Like others setting out on a journey, Saul did not know what would happen before that journey would come to an end. What was to happen on the road to Damascus was to change, not only the life of Saul, but the history of the world.

Travelling northwards, Saul would probably have crossed to the east side of the Jordan near the Sea of Galilee. From there he would have headed to the east of north, up into the wilderness of Damascus. He, and the temple police who no doubt rode with him, would have been guided by the snow capped peaks of Mount Hermon. Their destination lay to the east of the mountain. Then they were near Damascus, an oasis in the wilderness, full of fruit and flowers, kept green by the river Abana. But before they had reached the city, he who had planned to lay hands on believers was himself laid hold of by their Lord.

Although it was the middle of the day, it seemed as if lightning flashed around the travellers. Then a voice spoke. (Those travelling with Saul saw the light but not the person whose presence it announced; they heard a voice but could not make out the words.) He who had ridden in his own strength and in the assurance of the rightness of his cause fell to the earth, and his companions fell with him.

The glory was dazzling, but it was even more the grace of Jesus which was revealed to Saul that day. Saul had lived till then in a world of the law, in an atmosphere of legalism. He was fanatically devoted to the law. He took it as a personal insult when people like Stephen were reported as being opposed to the law (6:13). But the grace which he encountered outside Damascus was something from another world.

First, Jesus did not denounce him. He called him by his own name, twice. Then he asked him a question. Both the name and the question communicated a sense of Saul's value as a person. Next, Jesus introduced himself to Saul in a very personal way. He did not use some impersonal title, like 'Judge'; he said, *I am Jesus*. Then he indicated that, although Saul was indifferent to the sufferings of believers, Jesus cared about them. Their sufferings were his sufferings. The next thing which Jesus said must have been totally incomprehensible to someone as self-centred as Saul was, 'It is hard for you to kick against the goads' (Acts 26:14). As an animal who disobeys the prompting of a ploughman gets a sharp stick in its rear end, so Saul could only make trouble for himself by rebelling against Christ's rule. Saul's sin was causing him suffering and Jesus communicated to Saul the fact that he was concerned about that.

Saul's eyes were beginning to open spiritually. But the impact of this encounter was such that, when he rose from the earth, he physically could not see. He who had hoped to drag prisoners out of Damascus had himself to be led into the city. He was in a state of shock, and in this state he remained for three days, neither eating nor drinking. No doubt many passages of Scripture with which he had been familiar since childhood came to his mind during this period. He had used his knowledge of Scripture to support his rejection of Jesus. How could he understand these

Scriptures, now that Jesus had been revealed to him as Lord? And what about his sin of self-righteousness, and his cruelty towards believers? But what must have broken him down most of all during these three days was the gentleness of Jesus. He had heard a voice from the world of love – a world to which he was a stranger, but the world in which Jesus was Lord.

Think about it:

1. A modern conversion which shows remarkable parallels to Saul's was that of Sundar Singh in 1904: '... As I prayed and looked into the light, I saw the form of the Lord Jesus Christ. It had such an appearance of glory and love .... It was the Lord Jesus Christ, whom I had been insulting a few days before .... I heard a voice saying in Hindustani, "How long will you persecute me? I have come to save you, you are praying to know the right way. Why do you not take it?" ... So I fell at his feet and got this wonderful peace which I could not get anywhere else. This is the joy I was wishing to get. When I got up, the vision had all disappeared, but although the vision disappeared the peace and joy have remained with me ever since.'[19]

The conversion of Saul and of Sundar Singh were very dramatic, but a conversion does not have to be dramatic to be real. We do not need the drama of the conversion of Saul or of Sundar Singh. What we do need is the same Jesus as they met, and the same grace as they received through faith in him.

2. Saul's conversion reminds us that it is one thing to be religious, but another thing to be a Christian. Saul was full of religion when he set out on the road to Damascus. But this

was more of a hindrance than a help. He had to be emptied
of his religion, in order to be filled with Christ and his Spirit.

The conversion of George Whitefield, the famous evangelist of the eighteenth century, also illustrates this point. As
a student at Oxford, he was leading a very religious life
when he came across a book through which 'God showed
me that I must be born again or be damned. I learned that a
man may go to church, say his prayers, receive the sacrament, and yet not be a Christian. How did my heart rise and
shudder, like a poor man that is afraid to look into his
account books, lest he should find himself a bankrupt .... In
reading a few lines further that "true religion is a union of the
soul with God, and Christ formed within us," a ray of divine
light was instantaneously darted in upon my soul, and from
that moment, but not till then, did I know that I must become
a new creature.'[20]

Pray about it:
1. We may know people who are gifted, as Saul was, but
who are so sunk in sin and so enmeshed in false religion that
we cannot summon up enough faith to pray for their conversion. Saul's conversion should be a lasting warning to us,
against such unbelief. Remember how Augustine, too, was
apparently lost to immorality and heresy. Yet his mother,
Monica, wept on and prayed on. After his conversion in 386
Augustine wrote, joyfully parting from his past life, 'How
sweet did it at once become to me, to want (*be without*) the
sweetness of those toys! What I feared to be parted from was
now a joy to part with.'[21]

2. Believers are described here as being people of 'the Way'.
Later on, the gospel is described as 'the way of the Lord'

(18:25) and 'the way of salvation' (16:17). No doubt all these references stem originally from Jesus' own words in John 14:6, 'I am the way'.

Could we be described as people of 'the Way'? Is it our chief concern to live as those who follow Jesus? Pray that your thinking, your living and your talking will be sufficiently simplified and straightened out that you think, live and talk 'the Way'.

31. Received into the Church

Real prayer

In Damascus there was a disciple named Ananias. The Lord called to him in a vision, 'Ananias!' 'Yes, Lord,' he answered. The Lord told him, 'Go to the house of Judas on Straight Street and ask for a man from Tarsus named Saul, for he is praying. In a vision he has seen a man named Ananias come and place his hands on him to restore his sight' (Acts 9:10-12).

As with Saul, Jesus knew Ananias' name. This man who was to be the first to receive Saul of Tarsus into the Christian church may not have been famous on earth, but his name was known in heaven. When he heard his name Ananias said, 'Here I am, Lord'. He was like a soldier coming to attention at the approach of a superior officer. He was a disciple and he was ready to follow his Lord, wherever he might lead.

The directions which he received were very precise. He was given details of the street, the house, and the individual whom he was to visit. (Note the contrast between the brief, general directions given to Saul in verse 6 and the precise directions given to Ananias in verse 11. Saul may well have wished to know more, but God only gives us enough guidance for us to follow him. We do not get any more detail than we need.)

And Ananias was given the reason for this visit: 'He is praying.' What a change, from the picture presented in verse 1 of a serial killer! What a change, too, from the self-centred, ritualistic form of prayer to which Saul as an extreme Pharisee had been devoted till now! Here was real prayer.

Chosen by Jesus

'Lord,' Ananias answered, 'I have heard many reports about this man and all the harm he has done to your saints in Jerusalem. And he has come here with authority from the chief priests to arrest all who call on your name.' But the Lord said to Ananias, 'Go! This man is my chosen instrument to carry my name before the Gentiles and their kings and before the people of Israel. I will show him how much he must suffer for my name' (Acts 9:13-16).

Ananias gave two reasons why he was reluctant to visit Saul. First, Saul had an established reputation as a persecutor of the church. Second, the reason why Saul had made this one hundred and fifty mile trip up from Jerusalem was to drag believers off to prison. (In giving these reasons, Ananias incidentally expresses in two ways what it means to be a Christian. A Christian is a 'saint' – set free from sin and set apart to God. A Christian is also someone who calls on the name of the Lord. Both these points are picked up in 1 Corinthians 1:2, where Paul writes to 'the church of God which is at Corinth, to those who are sanctified in Christ Jesus, called to be saints, with all who in every place call on the name of Jesus Christ our Lord, both theirs and ours.')

Ananias had his reservations, but Jesus told him to get going and do what he had been told to do. Ananias really had no option anyway. As Jesus told him, Saul had already seen in a vision a man named Ananias coming to visit him! But Jesus did give Ananias some explanation of how important his mission to Saul was.

Saul would have been the church's last choice, but he had been chosen by Jesus. He was to be a vessel which would carry this most precious cargo – the revelation of the glory and the grace of God in Jesus Christ. And his special sphere of service had also been settled. He was to bring the gospel to the Gentiles. As Saul himself was afterwards to write: 'Although I am less than the least of all God's people, this grace was given me: to preach to the Gentiles the unsearchable riches of Christ' (Ephesians 3:8).

And Jesus did add a further note, perhaps to elicit Ananias' sympathy. He who had inflicted so much suffering on the church would himself yet know all about suffering for Christ. Not that Ananias was to tell Saul about this. Jesus himself would tell him, when he needed to know.

'Brother Saul ....'

> Then Ananias went to the house and entered it. Placing his hands on Saul, he said, 'Brother Saul, the Lord – Jesus, who appeared to you on the road as you were coming here – has sent me so that you may see again and be filled with the Holy Spirit.' Immediately, something like scales fell from Saul's eyes, and he could see again. He got up and was baptised, and after taking some food, he regained his strength (Acts 9:17-19a).

It is difficult to imagine Ananias' feelings, as he made his way across Damascus to Straight Street, found the house of Judas and entered the room in which Saul of Tarsus was. The lamb seeking the lion; the family of the victim seeking out the murderer. But the man in the corner of the room was a pathetic creature, blind and broken. What did Ananias feel as he crossed the room – rage, smouldering resentment, or a temptation to despise a bully who had met his match? Whatever he was tempted to feel, Ananias reached out to show Saul the most remarkable love.

He greeted him: '*Brother* Saul ....' And, as Jesus had touched untouchable lepers, Ananias reached out to touch this man who had been a monster. By that greeting and by that touch a whole world of wicked actions was loved away into oblivion.

Then Ananias spoke of what had happened to Saul on the road, and of why he had come to visit him. What was Saul's state of mind by this time? He could well have been at breaking point. In shock, weakened by the lack of food and drink, he could well have been asking himself: 'Did these things really happen? Was that really Jesus whom I met? How can I expect any follower of the Way to believe that he who is himself the Way appeared to me! Was I hallucinating in the heat of the midday sun?'

Ernest Hemingway wrote about an exciting experience he had while fishing off the coast of Cuba in 1934. To see a whale in that area was practically unknown, but Hemingway and his crew ran into a school of them. With completely inadequate equipment they tried to get in close enough to harpoon one of the whales. If they succeeded, they would be the proudest crew sailing into Havana that evening.

When their boat was twenty feet away from one of the whales, Hemingway fired the harpoon at its huge diving head. The harpoon only took hold briefly, then came away. The crew were bitterly disappointed at the loss of what, to them, would have been a fortune. They comforted themselves with the thought that, at least they could boast to their friends about this once-in-a-lifetime experience. They had the photographs to prove it.

But that was the problem. The man who was supposed to be taking of photographs had made a mess of it. Either he had shot into the sun or his hand had trembled with excitement, or there was so much water from the whale diving that the photograph looked as if it had been taken from the inside of a waterfall! 'We all knew,' Hemingway wrote, 'that his failure with the camera would make liars out of us for the rest of our lives. When something like that happens nobody believes you .... It was hard for me to believe it myself.'[22]

This could have been Saul's problem, too. He certainly had no photographic evidence to prove his unbelievable claim. But Saul did not even need to tell his story, wondering whether the members of the church would believe him or laugh at him. God comforted him by sending one of these believers to confirm to him what had happened on the road to Damascus without his having to say a word!

Instead of this visitor being sceptical, threatening to take away what Saul had received, he was the means of confirming the blessing which had come to him. Saul's sight was restored, God's Spirit was bestowed, and Saul was formally received into the church through the sacrament of baptism.

32. The End of the Beginning

The commencement of Saul's career

> Saul spent several days with the disciples in Damascus. At once he began to preach in the synagogues that Jesus is the Son of God. All those who heard him were astonished and asked, 'Isn't he the man who raised havoc in Jerusalem among those who call on this name? And hasn't he come here to take them as prisoners to the chief priests? Yet Saul grew more and more powerful and baffled the Jews living in Damascus by proving that Jesus is the Christ (Acts 9:19b-22).

The first miracle here is that Saul was *with* the believers at Damascus. The lion had joined the lambs.

The second miracle is that he spoke *for* them. Before his conversion, if Saul had heard a believer testify that Jesus was the Son of God, he would have crammed that testimony back down the believer's throat. Now that he had himself witnessed the glory of Jesus, Saul's voice became the strongest in the church in Damascus, testifying to the fact that Jesus is God's Son. Saul is not the only case of the persecutor turned preacher in the history of the church, but he is perhaps the most remarkable. 'He who formerly persecuted us now preaches the faith which he once tried to destroy' (Galatians 1:23).

People were naturally astounded by this turn in events. But, whatever people thought, Saul's testimony became increasingly powerful. As had been the case with Stephen (6:10), his opponents were unable to mount any effective opposition. Saul did have outstanding knowledge of the Scriptures, he was blessed with extraordinary gifts, and he could bring all his knowledge and gifts to bear with remarkable single-mindedness on whatever project he undertook. But the ultimate reason why he was able to silence opposition was that, to an ever increasing degree, the power of God flowed through him.

Escape from Damascus

> After many days had gone by, the Jews conspired to kill him, but Saul learned of their plan. Day and night they kept close watch on the city gates in order to kill him. But his followers took him by night and lowered him in a basket through an opening in the wall (Acts 9:23-25).

Luke does not mention the fact but, in his letter to the Galatians, Saul tells us that he visited Arabia around this time (Galatians 1:17). He need not have travelled very far; the border lay not many miles to the east of Damascus.

When he returned to Damascus, the Jews resolved to get rid of Saul. In this decision, they were supported by the 'governor' (2 Corinthians 11:32). Damascus was the capital of Syria, a province under Roman rule. But the king of Arabia appears to have had this local representative in Damascus. It is often thought that the purpose in Saul's visit to Arabia was to give him time to reflect quietly after the trauma of his life-changing encounter with Christ. This may have been the case. However, if Saul only spent his time in Arabia in quiet meditation, why did the representative of the Arabian king become involved in a plot to kill him? It seems likely that Saul spent at least part of his time in Arabia evangelising, and that this upset the authorities there.

Soldiers under the governor guarded the gates, and Jews

watched with them. But even as they watched the gates, a large basket appeared at the window of a house built on the city wall. The basket was lowered to the ground, and Saul escaped into the night.

Rejected in Jerusalem

When he came to Jerusalem, he tried to join the disciples, but they were all afraid of him, not believing that he really was a disciple. But Barnabas took him and brought him to the apostles. He told them how Saul on his journey had seen the Lord and that the Lord had spoken to him, and how in Damascus he had preached fearlessly in the name of Jesus. So Saul stayed with them and moved about freely in Jerusalem, speaking boldly in the name of the Lord. He talked and debated with the Grecian Jews, but they tried to kill him. When the brothers learned of this, they took him down to Caesarea and sent him off to Tarsus (Acts 9:26-30).

Jesus said that he would show to Saul the sufferings he would have to bear (v. 15). By now, Saul had learned what one part of these sufferings were to be – attempts made by those outside the church to kill him. Now Saul learned about another aspect of these sufferings – rejection by those within the church.

It was not as if Saul was merely being treated cautiously in the period immediately after his conversion. He tells us in Galatians 1:18 that it was after three years that he went up to Jerusalem. Following the Jewish way of reckoning, Saul could mean one complete year together with a brief part of the year before and of the year after. But even that length of time was surely enough for the church in Jerusalem to make up its mind. Paul was afterwards to write in 1 Corinthians

13:7 that love 'believes all things, hopes all things'. But there were those at the centre of the church in Jerusalem who did not have enough of that love. 'They were all afraid of him, not believing that he really was a disciple.'

It took strenuous efforts on the part of Barnabas to get Saul accepted in the Jerusalem church. Barnabas was the type of man who thinks of others. He had shown that already by selling a field and laying the proceeds at the apostles' feet, to meet the needs of those worse off than himself (Acts 4:36-37).

Luke states that Barnabas brought Saul to the apostles. But Saul himself says that at this stage he did not meet any of the leaders in Jerusalem except Peter and James, the Lord's brother (Galatians 1:18-19). How does this fit in with Luke's account, given that James was not strictly an apostle? Perhaps the sense is that, through meeting Peter and James, Saul was personally introduced to those who were effectively leading the church in Jerusalem. From James, Saul would have heard first hand about Jesus' early, private years. From Peter, he would have obtained graphic accounts of Jesus' public ministry.

Whatever initial rebuff Saul received from the church in Jerusalem he used his time there effectively, fulfilling his calling to preach the gospel. Stephen, in whose death Saul had been involved, had made a special effort to evangelise Grecian Jews in Jerusalem (6:9). Saul now followed Stephen's example, carrying on the work which had been cut short by Stephen's death. But the Grecian Jews responded to Saul's evangelistic efforts just as they had done when Stephen had sought to reach them. They tried to kill him.

At this stage Saul had a vision of Jesus, who warned him

that the people of Jerusalem would not receive his message
and that he should leave to concentrate on preaching the
gospel to the Gentiles (Acts 22:17f.). But there was also
another side to this. The members of the church in Jerusalem, hearing of the plots to kill Saul, were concerned to
shepherd him away from this danger. They took him to
Caesarea on the coast, and put him on a boat which was
headed north for Tarsus, Saul's home town.

Growth

> Then the church throughout Judea, Galilee and Samaria en-
> joyed a time of peace. It was strengthened; and encouraged by
> the Holy Spirit, it grew in numbers, living in the fear of the
> Lord (Acts 9:31).

Saul's next appearance in Luke's account comes in Acts
11:25, when Barnabas goes to Tarsus to find him. Between
Acts 9:30 and 11:25 there is a gap of eight or ten years.
Whatever Saul was doing during this period, Luke presents
the church as enjoying a time of quiet and steady growth.
This growth was outward, but also inward. It was quantita-
tive, but it was also qualitative.

Saul had been the main force behind the persecution of
the church, following on Stephen's death. Now that Saul
was converted, the church had rest. Luke mentions two
aspects of the life of the church. First of all, believers were
afraid to offend the Lord. (This makes one think of Chrysostom, patriarch of the church in Constantinople, who died
in 407 AD. When it was clear that the Roman Emperor
would act against him, Chrysostom was asked if he was not
afraid. His reply was, 'I fear only sin'.) Secondly, they
enjoyed the deep comfort of the Holy Spirit. As these two

apparently conflicting forces worked in the hearts of believers, they were built up. The quality of their spiritual life, which already was outstanding, improved even more.

This was clearly a significant point in the development of the early church. Saul, the immediate source of the church's harassment, had been taken out. Rather, he had been taken over by the grace of God. His heart and his life were to be laid down in God's service in such a way as would change the history of the world.

For the early church, seeking to establish itself in an alien world, it was not the beginning of the end. But it was, perhaps, the end of the beginning.

Think about it:
Saul must have found it deeply hurtful and discouraging that the church in Jerusalem was so reluctant to receive him. However, by the time that he came to write to the Galatians, he probably saw even that discouraging experience as working together for his good. Part of the background to the epistle seems to be that Saul had been accused of belonging to the Judaising section in the Jerusalem church. That was a group which insisted on maintaining, even in New Testament times, some of the outward rituals which belonged to the Old Testament period. In response to this accusation, Paul stated emphatically that he had not received his call to preach from anyone in Jerusalem but directly from God himself. In that situation it was helpful for Saul to be able to say that his early relationship with the leaders of the Jerusalem church was only a casual, and not an intimate one. It is better for us, too, to submit to whatever discouragements we may meet in God's service. We will usually find that they work together for good, as was the case with Saul.

Pray about it:
1. Some opponents of the early church were destroyed (see, for example, Acts 12:2, 3). But Saul was converted, so that the talents and dedication which had been devoted to the destruction of the church were then used for its advancement. We should pray for those whose talents are being used to oppose God's kingdom today, so that these same talents will instead come to be used for the good of others, and for the glory of God.

2. Are we, like Barnabas, more concerned to love than to be loved?

Ronald Dunn writes about a difficult time through which he was passing, and of how he felt depressed even when he and his family went away on holiday. Depression was like a miserable companion beside him every morning, waiting to accompany him through each day. Then, when he woke up one Thursday, the depression had gone. He knew of no reason for this until he went back to work and opened a letter which had arrived in his absence. It was from a friend who was intimately acquainted with the difficulties through which he was passing. While in prayer, this friend had felt led to minister to Ronald Dunn in a very special way: 'I have asked God to put on my heart as much burden as he can to lighten yours. I want to bear it with you.'[23] That letter was written at 3 am on the morning of the very day when Ronald Dunn felt that the burden had been lifted off his back!

Pray that God will guide you in how you minister to those whom you are called to support in God's service.

References

1. Soren Kierkegaard, 'The Journals' from *A Kierkegaard Anthology*, ed. Robert Bretall, Princeton University Press, 1946, p.10.
2. *I Believe,* George Carey, SPCK, 1991, p. 36.
3. Quoted in Carey, p. 37.
4. *Memoir and Remains of the Rev. Robert Murray McCheyne*, Andrew A. Bonar, 2nd Edn., 1892, p. 355.
5. See *The Book of Acts*, F. F. Bruce, Wm. B. Eerdmans Co., 1990, p. 41.
6. *What Happens When Women Pray?*, Evelyn Christenson, Scripture Press, 1992 edn., p. 28.
7. Christenson, p. 95-96.
8. *David Brainerd, His Life and Diary*, Moody Press, 1949, p. 216.
9. *All of Grace*, C. H. Spurgeon, Christian Focus Publications, p. 5.
10. *Covenanter Witness* (monthly publication of the Reformed Presbyterian Church of North America), May 1993, p. 13.
11. *The Burden is Light*, Eugenia Price, Fleming H. Revell Co., Spire edn., 1971, p. 74.
12. *Walking Back to Happiness,* Helen Shapiro, Harper Collins, 1994 edn., p. 275.
13. *Keep in Step With the Spirit*, J. I. Packer, IVP, 1984, p. 66.
14. *Dr. Kidd of Aberdeen*, James Stark, D. Wyllie & Son, 1898, p. 141.
15. *Ibid.* pp. 142-143.
16. *Concluding Unscientific Postscript*, Soren Kierkegaard., trans. Swenson and Lowrie, Princeton Univ. Press, 1941, p. 416.
17. *Festo Kivengere,* Anne Coomes, Monarch, pp. 397 and 380.
18. See *Herald* (magazine published by Christian Witness to Israel), Winter issue, 1993, p. 15.
19. B. H. Streeter and A.J. Appasamy, *The Sadhu,* London, 1921, pp 6-8, quoted in *The Book of Acts*, F. F. Bruce, p. 184.
20. *George Whitefield,* vol. 1, Arnold Dallimore, Banner of Truth Trust, 1970, p. 73.
21. *The Confessions of Saint Augustine*, trans. E. B. Pusey, The Medici Society, 1930, Book 9 (1).
22. *By-Line,* Ernest Hemingway, Ed. William White, Collins, 1968, p. 264.
23. *Don't Just Stand There ... Pray Something!*, Ronald Dunn, Scripture Press Foundation (UK) Ltd., 1993 edn., p. 87.

Commentaries consulted in the preparation of this book

The Acts of the Apostles, R. C. H. Lenski, Augsburg Publishing House, Minneapolis, 1961.

Acts, I. Howard Marshall, IVP, Leicester, 1986.

The Book of the Acts, F. F. Bruce, Eerdmans, Grand Rapids, 1990.

Interpreting Acts, E. F. Harrison, Zondervan, Grand Rapids, 1986.

Acts, Simon J. Kistemaker, Baker Book House, Grand Rapids, 1990.

The Acts of the Apostles, J. A. Alexander, James Nisbet and Co., London, 1862.